LIVING *the*
GOD-BREATHED LIFE

DESTINY IMAGE BOOKS BY THOM GARDNER

The Healing Journey
Healing the Wounded Heart

LIVING *the* GOD-BREATHED LIFE

An Invitation to Rest at the Table

THOM GARDNER

DESTINY IMAGE. PUBLISHERS, INC.

P.O. Box 310, Shippensburg, PA 17257-0310

"Speaking to the Purposes of God for This Generation and for the Generations to Come."

This book and all other Destiny Image, Revival Press, MercyPlace, Fresh Bread, Destiny Image Fiction, and Treasure House books are available at Christian bookstores and distributors worldwide.

For a U.S. bookstore nearest you, call **1-800-722-6774.**

For more information on foreign distributors, call **717-532-3040.**

Reach us on the Internet: **www.destinyimage.com.**

ISBN 13 Trade Paper: 978-0-7684-3619-8

ISBN 13 Hardcover: 978-0-7684-3620-4

ISBN 13 Large Print: 978-0-7684-3621-1

ISBN 13 E-book: 978-0-7684-9047-3

For Worldwide Distribution, Printed in the U.S.A.

1 2 3 4 5 6 7 8 9 10 / 14 13 12 11

CONTENTS

FOREWORD

I f there is one thing both Scripture and history tell us, it is that life is a journey. The great stories of faith seem to always involve some transforming pilgrimage from "here to there." Along the way people were changed—often dramatically. Abram became Abraham as he made the long journey to the land of God's promise, transitioning from the son of Terah to the father of the nation of Israel. Joseph started out as a beloved son, then became an abused slave, and eventually rose to be the Minister of Egypt, all as part of his long and arduous journey of faith. Then there was Moses, the prince of Egypt, who was forged into the friend of God as he moved from bondage to the Promised Land, leading the people of God to the land of milk and honey. And what about Paul? His entire story is a tale of pilgrimage from persecutor to believer to the man possessed with Christ who pressed on in life toward one great goal—to be like Jesus.

All of life is a journey, and for the Christian there is but one ultimate destination. We are called to become like Jesus. Day by day, in big and small ways, the Holy Spirit is working to change us into the likeness of Christ. It is a work of grace accomplished by the Lord, yet it involves our surrender, to be sure. As every Christian knows, the landscape of that journey is quite varied. There are "mountains high and valleys low" and more than a few long days and dark nights.

Frankly, the journey of faith brings its share of victories and defeats. Anyone who has walked the path for even a short time knows that. There are blessings and gifts for sure, but the journey is not easy and not for the faint of heart. I have had my own share of hard knocks along the way and have faced some trials that caused me to question my survival. But through it all, the Lord has been there and has used every step along the way to bring change. Deep change. Important change. Necessary change.

Journeys happen best when someone is guiding you along the path—not just any someone, but rather a seasoned traveler who is well acquainted with the terrain, the challenges, and the demands you will face as you press forward toward Jesus Christ. Thom Gardner is just that sort of guide. He is well along the path himself and has his own stories of victory, defeat, blessing, and trial. Because of that, Thom Gardner has something to offer as we make the journey toward Jesus Christ.

This book, like so many of Thom's books, is a rich combination of Scripture, sound interpretation, practical guidance, and sensitivity to the needs of people who sometimes feel weak and wounded, like me. It is map for the journey, a "pilgrim's" handbook, and a survival guide all rolled into one. It is a rare resource that has one foot firmly planted in the Word and the other carefully placed in real time and space. There is a richness to the people Thom introduces us to, both from the pages of Scripture and from the experiences of brothers and sisters walking with us today. And Thom helps us understand our own stories as well. He wants us to see that our stories are about us and Jesus—being with Jesus, growing close to Jesus, and becoming like Jesus.

Simply stated, life is a journey toward Christ. This book will help you move further along that path. I recommend it to you wholeheartedly.

—Dr. Terry Wardle
Ashland Theological Seminary

Appetizer

Since before our marriage, Carol and I have had this thing about being at the table. Even before the days I walked as a disciple of Jesus Christ, we spent time at the table. We used to cook together when we were dating. My neighbors probably thought I was running a restaurant as the fragrance of stuffed rigatoni and garlic wafted through the door. Mmmmm!

The table has always been a part of us somehow. We lived for a period of more than 20 years in a small three-bedroom house on Warm Spring Road in Chambersburg, Pennsylvania. We raised two of our girls there. It was a very simple home with an attached dining room that had many windows. At night the light shone out of that little dining room whose predominant feature was a table. Many people from princes to prophets came to that little house and that table. Now and then someone would stop by who had run out of gas or who had some other kind of need. Once or twice we would be sitting there praying or talking with someone when a car would pull over, and someone would ask us to pray for them. It was always a puzzlement why strangers would stop. After all, there was nothing distinguishing about that little house. It was a small white-framed rancher with brickwork half the way up and a fence that gathered in the backyard to keep the kids and the two little dogs in order.

One evening, or rather early morning, Carol got up to answer the door at something like 3:00 A.M. I was unconscious and did not even hear the doorbell. When Carol answered the door, a young lady was there who was quite intoxicated. Carol brought her to the table in the dining room and made her some coffee. The young woman, who was essentially homeless, had been abandoned along the road and didn't know where she was or much of anything else for that matter. Carol talked with her for an hour or so and I finally woke up, got myself together, and came to the table with them. Of course Carol had her whole story by that time.

As I joined them at the table, we talked and prayed with her for a short time and then drove her to a motel where she had been staying with someone. As I parked the car to let the young lady out I asked her, "Sister, why did you pick our house to stop this morning?" Our house was very small and nothing special. The young woman replied, "It was the only house with a light on." I believe it was because the table was set.

Through many years in that little house, many people came to our table. Some came for prayer; some came for Carol's great waffles at breakfast or some other meal. We drank gallons of coffee at that table and washed it with many tears. Sometimes we brought young folks home from the music store we owned and operated for several years. A few came to Christ by hanging out in the music store in the Jesus-filled atmosphere that was cultivated there. It was a retail store, but many of the folks who worked with me there were believers. Looking back I see that the folks who hung around were looking for a place at the table—any table. A few of the young folks that came to our home burned their heavy-metal recordings in the back yard. There may still be a black spot there somewhere behind the shed.

In the end, the retail music store we operated failed. While it was running, we never set out to have or be in any kind of ministry. We just set the table and people came. We still do.

The table is still important to us as a venue for connection and ministry where everything gets warm and simple. We raised our children at that table. I sometimes studied Hebrew with my late friend Rabbi Gilner at that table. A few folks came to know Jesus at that table, not because of anything we said, but because they were loved there.

I have come to see that there has never been a more spiritual activity than sitting around the table and loving people face-to-face. The table was and is a plane of compassion and an expression of the Kingdom of God. The table is where God and people can be near to us—sitting right across from us so we can see them face-to-face. It is the place of vulnerability, sharing, intimacy, transformation, and much more. It is the place where we are present to each other, and all the weapons of daily warfare and emotional defense are laid aside at the door while dinner is on.

In this humble little writing, we are going on a journey together with Christ. In Part One, "The Conversation," we will join the journey with the first two followers whom Jesus brought to His table. We will experience our abiding in Christ. This is the journey of *conformation*.

In Part Two, "The Table," we will once again be joining followers of Jesus on a road to a table at Emmaus. Our table will become *His* table. Jesus will take the bread of our lives into His hands and bless it. Here Christ abides in us. This is the journey of *transformation.*

In the final part of this book, "The Encounter," you will experience a personal journey—a coming to the table with Christ. This is the ongoing journey of personal healing and *simplification* in the presence of Christ.

Beloved one, Jesus and a fuller knowledge of His life awaits us as we journey together with Him to the table. It is the abundant life Jesus promised to us. It is the life of *becoming* where we come to His table carrying only an invitation. It is a life of rest where it is no longer I who live, but Christ who lives in me and through me (see Gal. 2:20). It is *Living the God-Breathed Life.*

PART I

THE CONVERSATION

Before the miracles—before all the amazing words of Jesus' teaching—came a simple conversation. The words of this conversation are as fresh and as central today as they were two thousand years ago when Jesus walked among us in human form. This simple three-line conversation touches every area of our lives—every decision from how we invest our time and money to how we raise our kids. These are the first words of Jesus the Messiah, an initiation into the heart of His mission. These words, carried across the dust of time, determine the peace, power, and presence of God we experience as we join with Jesus and His first two followers along the way.

CHAPTER ONE

WHAT DO YOU SEEK?

...John was standing with two of his disciples, and he looked at Jesus as He walked, and said, "Behold, the Lamb of God!" The two disciples heard him speak, and they followed Jesus. And Jesus turned and saw them following, and said to them, "What do you seek?" (John 1:35-38a)

THE JOURNEY

There were two of us standing in the water with John that day—a day that began like most other days. Crowds of people from various parts of the country came to John to be immersed in the Jordan, to wash away the guilt of sin in hope of a new beginning. John was a man of the desert, barefooted and clothed in a rough garment of camel hair held fast by a crude leather belt. He was an intense and focused man. Though He was focused on his mission of repentance, his eyes often looked up out of the water to watch for the arrival of the Coming One of whom he often spoke. John had no belongings to speak of, no riches or official position, yet he spoke with authority so moving that everyone from the rustic to the religious listened to his words about the coming reign of God.

Like the other seekers, we left behind home and life as we knew it, seeking something more of God, which led us now to this barefooted wanderer in camel hair. Now, late in the day, another solitary figure approached. Nothing about His appearance set Him apart, yet His presence seemed to reach us before He did. There was no mistaking that He was a son of Abraham, but His bearing and appearance were unlike most rabbis and preachers of the time. He was a tradesman—a carpenter. He was powerfully built. His face was tanned and leathery from the sun, and His hands were layered with calluses, just like any other man who worked for a living handling wood and stone. No one but John seemed to be impressed with His arrival. No one else was looking for Him.

Now, lifting his hand to shield his eyes from the late afternoon sun, John looked at the man and announced clearly, *"This is the One—This is the Lamb of God!"* The Baptizer spoke loud enough for those of us close by to hear. He paid little attention to the religious types clothed in long formal robes who came to trap him with their questions of messiahs and prophets. They stood at a safe distance, bending their ears and straining toward John to hear what he was saying. They wouldn't have gotten it anyway.

Now the Lamb was not a man who stood meekly by, but one headed in a definite direction. I cannot recall if He actually stopped at all. He continued on His way west toward Capernaum, walking with determined steps.

John turned to us, stepping back and out of the way, gesturing a few times with his head and hand that we should go after the Lamb whose back we could see as He continued on His way. We had to hurry to catch up to the Lamb. Water dripped off of us as we struggled to reattach our sandals and pull up our garments to follow after the Lamb. We were walking quickly into the late afternoon sun which silhouetted the figure of the Lamb who walked ahead of us.

As we followed the Lamb, the descending sun and cooler air reminded us that it was getting late and that the Rest was near. We needed to find a place to keep the Shabbat as our fathers were told generations before—a place to connect with the God of Israel. Each step carried us farther away from all that felt usual and safe and closer to the Lamb. We had no food or extra clothing with us, no tools or other means to observe the approaching day of Rest. Wherever the Lamb was going would have to be a safe place for the night.

The Lamb, who we came to know as Jesus, seemed to know where He was going so we just followed Him. Just when we had gotten used to looking at the back of His head, He looked back over His shoulder, stopped, and turned fully around, looking at us eye-to-eye. With the sun at His back, Jesus looked at one of us then the other saying nothing. Then, with great tenderness and purpose, he asked us a simple question. *"What do you seek?" "What are you looking for?"* The words struck deep within me.

I didn't know quite what to say. It was a simple and obvious question, but it left me standing flatly on my feet. My friend and I looked at each other as if the answer should have been obvious. After all, we were faithful followers of John and the way of holiness. Yet His question connected with a deep longing—an expectant emptiness that rose within me. It was a question no one had ever asked me, at least not in a way that I thought they really wanted to know my answer. He had not asked what we thought or how we should do something or an opinion on the Teachings. His question cut to the heart and became the only question. He had put us in pursuit of something more than another method or pathway. *What were we really looking for?*

WHAT DO YOU SEEK?

Step into the sandals of the first two followers of Jesus for a minute. Jesus spins around suddenly looking at you eye-to-eye with great tenderness and asks you, *"What do you seek?"* Jesus asked the same question many times when He encountered people with obvious healing needs. Jesus wasn't asking, "What do you like?" or

"Would you prefer chocolate, vanilla, or strawberry?" Jesus was not being insensitive or dull; He was asking what was important—what were they going after?

How would you answer Him? The very first words the son of God, the Messiah, spoke on planet earth to His disciples were a question—a life question. In fact, Jesus asked pretty much the same question of His parents in the temple when He was 12 years old. *"Why is it that you were looking for Me?"*[1]

Jesus asked the same question of folks who needed healing. He asked a man who lay around waiting for healing for more than 30 years, *"Do you wish to get well?"* (see John 5:1-9). Once He met a man who was obviously blind sitting outside of Jericho, and He walked right past him. Then the man called out, *"Jesus, son of David, have mercy on me."* Jesus stopped, turned around, and said to the crowd, *"Call him here."* The man jumped up and threw aside his only means of livelihood, his cloak, scattering coins and bits of food everywhere. We can almost see this man groping along the arms of the folks who had told him to shut up and put up with his blind state of being just moments before. When the beggar came to the face of Jesus, blind as ever, Jesus asked him, *"What do you want Me to do for you?"*—or in other words, *what do you seek?* The blind man replied, *"I want to regain my sight."* But there was a purpose beyond physical sight in the man's response. As soon as the man regained his sight, the Gospels tell us he began following Jesus. Now we know what he was seeking. He was seeking more than physical healing; he was seeking Jesus Himself (see Mark 10:46-52).

What do you seek? How would you answer Him? What are you looking for? What are you pursuing? What is important to you?

What do you feel is lost or missing from your life? Pretend that no one is watching you right now—that you are totally alone with your heart. How would you answer the question? When you look into the eyes of your children or grandchildren or your spouse or your faith community, *what are you seeking?* What are you looking for? What is lost to you?

This question and the answer to it determine our peace in every aspect of our life's journey, from our friends to our finances. Whatever we seek, whatever we are searching for drives and directs us. It becomes our operating system. Whatever I seek steals my heart. Jesus, describing the Kingdom of God, uses the example of a man who put everything on the line for what was important and of value to him. *"The kingdom of heaven is like a merchant seeking fine pearls, and upon finding one pearl of great value, **he went and sold all that he had** and bought it"* (Matt. 13:45-46). What are you and I selling ourselves for? What are we going after?

When I was a younger man and a professional trumpeter, I practiced many hours every day in addition to rehearsals. Music was a seductress inviting me to try and fill an emptiness, distracting me from emotional pain and inviting me to gain love through musical performance. I never got there. There was always another performance ahead and a higher note to be squeezed out. At the end, all I got was a headache. Others may seek a better career or more money. Maybe we sell ourselves just to be right in some argument or to even the score with someone who has hurt us. Whatever we seek costs us everything.

HOW DO WE KNOW WHAT WE SEEK?

How do we know what we're really seeking? The first place to start is to look around at our lives. What do we spend our money and energy on? What do we think about—dream about? What's in our checkbooks or on our calendars? What do we give our attention to? What kinds of voices do we listen to? What kinds of people do we hang out with? What books have we read in the last year? What do we allow to come into our homes and hearts through media? What are we willing to put up with? What moves our emotions? What do we talk about? What do we want for our children or grandchildren? What do we most complain about? What do we worry about? What do we count on to bring us peace? What can we not live without? What makes it a good day or a bad day for us? What's in our attics or basements that we just can't throw away? If we spend some serious time just meditating on those questions, we will get a good idea of what we seek.

Carol and I moved recently from a home we lived in for more than 20 years. We didn't realize how much stuff we had until we had to deal with it. As I was rummaging through the basement, I came across papers and notes from church meetings I had saved about a particularly hurtful conflict we had had with other leaders. It happened years before, yet I must have kept the files as evidence. How silly. I had not realized how much my heart was controlled by hurt and bitterness. I was seeking lost reputation and retaining evidence of my "rightness." I threw them into the trash where they belonged. I was seeking to be right, and that quest kept some part of my heart in unrest.

What we seek not only determines our lives, but also shapes our children and family for generations. In raising my own children, I have to say that, at the very least, I've been an imperfect and distracted follower of Jesus Christ.

Remember the rich young man who came to the feet of Jesus and asked, "How may I have eternal life?" Here was someone who had most of what the world wants—youth, wealth, and spirituality. Yet in all that, he came to Jesus empty and longing for something else to fill him. All the stuff and belongings left him emptier. You can almost hear Dr. Jesus say, *"How's that workin for ya?"* The young man needed something more eternal than anything he'd found up to that point.

Jesus answered, "Obey God's law," and the man replied that he had done all that since he was a child. But Jesus looked at the young man, eye-to-eye and filled with love, and said, "There is one thing missing. You need to examine what possesses you—what has a hold on you. Give up that stuff and follow Me to become what I am and be where I am" (see Mark 10:21-22). Note that this man did not ask, *"How do I get You, Jesus? How do I get a heart like Yours?"* It seems as though this young man wanted eternal life, but without the presence of the Lord Himself. How tragic.

SEEKING THE SEEKER

The Lord will never settle for top billing in our lives. He is not impressed with bumper stickers saying He is number One. He wants to be the *only* One! We seek first the Kingdom of God or, better yet, the King of that Kingdom before all (see Matt. 6:33). Paul wrote that Jesus is to have first place in all things (see Col. 1:18). Jesus Himself quoted the Torah saying, *"You shall worship the Lord your God and serve Him only"* (Luke 4:8). There is no second place in the pursuit of God. We don't just pursue Him harder than everything else. We seek Him only, and everything else flows to us as we go after God. *"Everything that goes into a life of pleasing God has been miraculously given to us by getting to know, personally and intimately, the One who invited us to God"* (2 Pet. 1:3 MSG).

In his inspired story, *The Shack*, William P. Young relates a conversation between God and Mack, his main character, who has been invited into greater and more personal depths of revelation in the heart of God at the table.

Jesus speaks to Mack and says:

> Mack, I don't want to be first among a list of values; I want to be at the center of everything...Rather than a pyramid, I want to be the center of a mobile, where everything in your life—your friends, family, occupation, thoughts, activities—is connected to me but moves in the wind, in and out and back and forth, in an incredible dance of being.[2]

As it turns out, Jesus is seeker-sensitive. He is seeking seekers. In the opening Scripture, John tells us that when Jesus became aware of the two following Him, He turned around. In fact we might better translate it that "Jesus became turned around." Something got His attention. Somehow Jesus could feel the two brothers pursuing Him, and it turned Him around to see them face-to-face, the very position from which Adam first saw his Creator as he was kissed alive (see Gen. 2:7).

Jesus said, *"The Son of Man has come to seek and to save that which was lost"* (Luke 19:10). Something or someone is lost. The word translated "lost" here could easily be translated "destroyed." Something has been destroyed, and Jesus was setting out to restore it.[3] What has been lost, what has been destroyed, is our intimate connection to the One who breathed us into being.

God is a Seeker and Creator without peer. It was longing in the heart of God that caused Him to cry out a succession of "Let there be's" to speak worlds into existence. And from the moment we turned away from the face of God to lesser things, He came tramping through the garden seeking us.

God is a "sensitive Seeker" who looks for those who are seeking after Him. The draw and desire for home in us connects with the heart of God and turns Him around to see us face-to-face. Our need and emptiness meets the desire of God to love and be loved. *"God is always on the alert, constantly on the lookout for people who are totally committed to Him..."* (2 Chron. 16:9 MSG). He is the Rewarder of those who seek Him with all they have (see Heb. 11:6). He is the Reward!

WHAT WE SEEK

We search the Scriptures or the Internet thinking they will bring us life, but what we really want, what we were created for, is to be filled with God—to be at home in Him. Our attempts to fill our emptiness with rubbish or religion are as ineffective as the attempts of those who trusted in John's ritual waters of baptism to make it to

Heaven. We seek God because there is something in us that tells us we might be filled by Him.

What do you seek? What are you pursuing? Where will these things or people lead you if you get them? Do they lead you Home? Whatever does not lead me closer to Home will lead me away from Him. If I'm not becoming more devoted, I will probably become more distracted.

> *...Truly, truly, I say to you, you seek Me, not because you saw signs, but because you ate of the loaves and were filled. Do not work for the food which perishes, but for the food which endures to eternal life, which the Son of Man will give to you, for on Him the Father, God, has set His seal* (John 6:26-27).

Something is moved in the heart of God for those who seek Him first. Nicodemus sought Jesus by night to see whether He might be the One who was to come. There was Nicodemus in all his religious garb and tradition—a man who, to the world, looked like he had God and salvation in the bag. Despite all his connections and convictions, something was missing—lost. He couldn't risk looking bad to the other religious folks, so he went to Jesus in the dark of night. (Nic at Night?) Jesus responded to this seeker with great affection. "Nicodemus, you have to seek Me in a totally new way, not according to the dead teaching of the Law, but in the Spirit. In fact, just like John, you will not even recognize me until you look beyond what you know now and seek Me personally. You were born for home. Come home" (see John 3:1-13).

There is only one thing we can seek that will ever satisfy and fill us. That is Christ, who must become our heart's petition. Listen to the seeking heart of David...

> *The one thing I ask of the Lord—the thing I seek most—is to live in the house of the Lord all the days of my life, delighting in the Lord's perfections and meditating in His Temple* (Psalm 27:4 NLT).

What are you and I seeking? We are seeking Home. We were born homesick. Deep inside of each one of us is a child who feels lost and longs for home. What is home to you? Home is where we are comfortable, where we can walk around the house in our bathrobes and slippers without fear. Home is where we relax in the familiarity of our dinner tables. Home is not necessarily a house. There are many who live in million dollar houses, but are effectively homeless. Right now, as I write these words, Carol and I are at the beach villa of dear friends. But when we are finished with our activities at the end of the day, we say we are "going home." Home is where we are together in intimate fellowship.

Our hearts long for a home and rest. This longing and seeking in our hearts is like a GPS, a "God Positioning System," which tells us how close or far we are from home. Sometimes we make a wrong turn in our search to fill this longing, but this GPS programmed by the mercy and longing of a Father's heart recalculates and vectors us toward home again.

Though we try to quiet our wild-seeking hearts with everything from pizza to piety, nothing outside of us will ever be able to still what begins on the inside. Calvin Miller writes, "When God does not fill the vacuum, a host of consuming appetites swarm through better intentions."⁴ And the One we long for wants us to find Him and to make His home in us. (See John 14:23.) Christ *is* Home!

You and I are seekers—seekers of Home. The One we seek, who seeks us, looks us in the eyes with tenderness and asks, *"What do you seek?"*

JOIN *the* JOURNEY

At this moment you have the attention of Heaven. Sit and take a deep breath with your eyes closed. Read the Scripture again to yourself out loud a few times.

> *Again the next day John was standing with two of his disciples, and he looked at Jesus as He walked, and said, "Behold, the Lamb of God!" The two disciples heard him speak, and they followed Jesus. And Jesus turned and saw them following, and said to them,* **"What do you seek?"** (John 1:35-38a)

As you meditate on these verses, close your eyes and put yourself in the place of those two seekers. Can you feel yourself walking closer to the Lord? As you draw closer, He becomes aware of your presence and turns around, seeing you face-to-face. Let yourself feel the drawing of His heart toward you and yours toward Him. The Lamb now turns to you and asks, "What do you seek? What are you after? What have you pursued that left you unsatisfied and empty? What has a hold on your life?" Where do you feel lost?

Here are a few questions to consider which may help you discover what you are looking for, though they are not the only questions.

- How do you spend your money?

_____

_____

_____

- How do you spend your time?

_____

_____

_____

- What are you chasing after?

_____

_____

- What makes a day good or bad for you?

_____

_____

- What do you give your attention to?

  _____

  _____

- Who or what do you trust?

  _____

  _____

- What brings you peace?

  _____

  _____

- What is important to you?

  _____

  _____

- What do you value?

  _____

  _____

- What do you think or daydream about?

_____

_____

Write below what comes to your mind. He may remind you of these things through mental images or any number of ways. Don't file through your own mind; let the Lord remind you. List whatever the Lord brings to mind and then lay those things down and leave them along the pathway as you continue to follow after Jesus.

_____

_____

_____

_____

_____

_____

_____

_____

_____

_____

_____

_____

Whatever you seek other than the Lord is not worthy to be compared with knowing Him. Where have you "come to" Jesus without "coming after" Him?

As you join the journey with Jesus, you are not sure where He is leading you quite yet. Are you willing to trust Him and seek Him in order to become like Him?

Pray this Scripture aloud in the personal presence of Jesus Christ.

> *Lord, as I join this journey with You, I confess: I once thought all these things were so very important, but now I consider them worthless because of what Christ has done. Yes, everything else is worthless when compared with the priceless gain of knowing Christ Jesus my Lord. I have discarded everything else, (left it along the path) counting it all as garbage, so that I may have Christ and become one with You* (see Philippians 3:7-9 NLT).

ENDNOTES

1. The same Greek word is used in both John 1:38 and Luke 2:49; *zeteo*, to seek or desire something. This Greek word is used many times in the Gospels with Jesus as the object.

2. William P. Young, *The Shack* (Newbury Park, CA: Windblown Media, 2007), 207.

3. The word translated "lost" is *apollumi*, which carries the image of something destroyed.

4. Calvin Miller, *Into the Depths of God* (Minneapolis, MN: Bethany House, 2001), 29.

CHAPTER TWO

WHERE DO YOU LIVE?

*Jesus turned, saw them following Him, and asked, "What are you looking for?" They answered, "**Where do You live**, Rabbi?" (This word means "Teacher.")* (John 1:38 TEV)

WHERE DO YOU LIVE?

As the Lamb asked us *what we were seeking,* our hearts settled into a simpler and sharper focus. His question caused more questions and we struggled for answers to erupt from our hearts. We wanted to ask, "Who are You?" "Where are You from?" "Are You the Messiah—the One John and we have been waiting for?"

Now as we stood face-to-face with the Lamb, all of the many questions that had turned over in our hearts slipped into the background and became one question: *"Rabbi, where are You going; where do You live?"* This was an important question. It was late, and wherever He was going we would have to go and stay there with Him for the Rest. If we were to follow Him, we would seek to become what He was.

Jesus looked at us now with greater intensity. As we watched Him consider our question, the corner of His eyes lifted up ever so slightly in a smile. There was excitement in His expression, as though He had been waiting for someone to ask just this question, *"Where do You live?"* His face and manner told us that this leg of the journey was going to be different—this was not about instruction in new rules or laws. This was going to be personal. *"Rabbi, where do You live?"*

WHERE WE LIVE

In the days of Jesus walking the dusty roads of Galilee, it was very common for students to choose a teacher or a rabbi to follow. The follower was invited to sit and "wallow in the dust at the rabbi's feet."[1] In other words, they would live close to him and hang on his words.

We usually think of disciples as people learning rules and laws. We wince at the word discipleship and associate it with a new religious paint job on the outside. My friend Dave Hess says we are always learning the rules of the swimming pool, but never jump in the pool. A disciple is a person who takes up the life of the one they follow to become what they are. Disciples are "becomers." It has been popular to ask, "What would Jesus do?" But a becomer asks, "Where does Jesus live?"

When we live close to someone, it changes us. John the Baptist said of Jesus, "Jesus, I have to be more like You and less like myself" (see John 3:30). We become like the folks we hang out with. Some folks say that married couples grow to look like one another after years of marriage. (Fortunately, Carol has been spared this.) The longer we live together, the more our hearts grow together. The longer we are married, the better I know where she *lives* and what her heart needs. I value things she values and vice versa (though I still don't like liver and brussels sprouts).

As we ask Jesus, "Where do You live?" we are entering into a relationship of trust.[2] To transition from *seeker* to *becomer,* we must go beyond meeting our needs or answering questions and take up the life of the One we follow. An old *becomer* said it this way: "...Whoever wants to understand the words of Christ and fully and slowly savor their sweetness has to work hard at making himself another Christ."[3] Therefore, to become a disciple is to become all that Jesus is in heart, character, and mission. Oswald Chambers wrote...

...Discipleship means personal, passionate devotion to a Person—our Lord Jesus Christ....To be a disciple is to be a devoted bondservant motivated by love for the Lord Jesus.[4]

True intimacy—living closely with Christ—transforms us. We become different people. Our present idea of intimacy with God has become a vague emotional squishiness rather than radical transformation in His presence. We see intimacy with God like a date with candy and flowers and a kiss at the door at the end of the night. The Lord is seeking more than a date or a diversion. He wants all of us. Christ wants me to live so closely that His aftershave, Ancient of Days Spice, is on me.

It's not enough for us to master the rules—to do the right things or not do the wrong things. If I live close to the Lord, I will do what pleases Him. Life is not about walking on eggshells hoping not to make a deadly mistake, but about living closely and learning to know the person of Jesus. Jesus said, *"This is the work of God, that you believe* [trust] *in Him whom He has sent"* (John 6:29). Jesus came to bring joy, not a joystick to control us like a video game! Obedience comes from abiding in His presence and love. Listen to these words.

> *If you keep My commandments, you will abide in My love; just as I have kept My Father's commandments and abide in His love. These things I have spoken to you so that My joy may be in you, and that your joy may be made full* (John 15:10-11).

We have the same relationship with Jesus that He had with the Father during His life on Earth—a relationship based on *abiding*, which leads to *love* resulting in *joy*. First comes love in devotion, then comes the obedience. No matter how I translate this verse, I cannot see Jesus driven with fear and trembling into the presence of the Father. I see a Son who draws near and whose heart becomes like Abba's. More than anything else, Jesus wanted us to be one in heart with Him as He was with the Father (see John 17:22).

There is an active "get out of the way" kind of pursuit happening when we ask the Lord, "Where do You live?" King David, a man who knew something about going after the heart of God, said, "...

Seek peace and pursue it" (Ps. 34:14). This is not just a searching for something missing; it is an all-out pursuit for peace, which can only be found in the presence of the Prince of Peace, Jesus Christ.[5] David wanted to be where God was—to live where He lived. David and the Son of David had a relationship of total devotion with the Father. As we move from *"seeker"* to *"becomer,"* we will move from obsession to devotion.

I recall the first sight I had of my wife Carol. I was managing a music store and looking for someone to teach flute students. Carol was teaching many private students in the area, and I called her to see if she would be interested in teaching for us. I remember the first sight of her as she walked into the music store. I can still hear the sound of the bell jingling over the door as she opened it and I got my first look at her. She had my complete attention. By some miracle that I still don't understand, she agreed to have a cup of coffee with me though I was at the bottom of life at that time. We married a couple years later. (She never did teach flute lessons in the store.)

What attracted me to Carol at first was her physical beauty. At first I didn't know her or her heart, and I really wasn't much concerned about anything other than myself. It was all about me. I was obsessed with her, not devoted.

Obsession and devotion are worlds apart. In human relation-ships, obsession is about *me* and devotion is about *you*. I have often counseled folks who are obsessed with their spouses instead of devoted to them. Obsession is the root of abuse. To abuse is to *abnormally use* someone to meet our own needs. I once had several sessions with a couple who were at the point of splitting up because the wife wanted to restyle her hair. Restyle her hair!! They were from a very conservative religious culture, and the husband was afraid what others in his conservative family would say about the new style. It was all about him and what the family would think.

Nowhere in the Scriptures are we told to be obsessed with God, but instead to be devoted or to serve God with a whole heart. Listen to David's last words to his son Solomon:

> *As for you, my son Solomon, know the God of your father, and* **serve Him with a whole heart** *and a willing mind; for the Lord searches all hearts, and understands every intent of the thoughts. If you seek Him, He will let you find Him...* (1 Chronicles 28:9).

Another way to put it is the difference between coming *to* Christ and coming *after* Christ. As a seeker obsessed with meeting my own needs, I may come *to* Christ as my problem-solver. In other words, I follow Christ so that He will heal me or save me or guide me. To be sure, the Lord heals us and provides for us because He loves us, not because we have Him over a Scriptural barrel.

Thomas á Kempis wrote:

> *...Many people are self-seekers; that's to say it is themselves they are chasing, and they don't even know it. They seem happy enough when things are going their way. But when they aren't, they run and sit in a corner and cry big tears.*[6]

We have had a rash of self-seeking Christianity in recent history; we've seen God's whole purpose as serving us. Paul's description of the Church two thousand years ago reflects the carnality and obsession of the modern Church as well, especially in America.

> *For men will be lovers of self, lovers of money, boastful, arrogant, revilers, disobedient to parents, ungrateful, unholy, unloving, irreconcilable, malicious gossips, without self-control, brutal, haters of good, treacherous, reckless, conceited, lovers of pleasure rather than lovers of God, holding to a form of godliness, although they have denied its power...* (2 Timothy 3:2-5).

Devotion is a different matter altogether. To be devoted is to be consumed by the One to whom we are devoted. We have made holiness about what we do or what we wear or how we speak. But holiness is not about what we *do;* it's about where we *live!* To be devoted is to belong to Christ—to be holy—to live where He lives.[7]

Devotion is about closeness. In ancient Israel the priests were anointed with fragrant oil, and they walked through the incense with its cinnamon and cassia. They smelled like God! They lived where Yahweh lived. When we are devoted to Christ, we carry His fragrance to the world.

Paul said that he put everything in the trash barrel for the purpose of knowing Christ: desires, accomplishments, titles, degrees (see Phil. 3:8,10). It's all about knowing Christ and being where He is. I like the way The Message put this:

The very credentials these people are waving around as something special, I'm tearing up and throwing out with the trash—along with everything else I used to take credit for. And why? Because of Christ. Yes, all the things I once thought were so important are gone from my life. Compared to the high privilege of knowing Christ Jesus as my Master, firsthand, everything I once thought I had going for me is insignificant—dog dung. I've dumped it all in the trash so that I could embrace Christ and be embraced by him. I didn't want some petty, inferior brand of righteousness that comes from keeping a list of rules when I could get the robust kind that comes from trusting Christ—God's righteousness. I gave up all that inferior stuff so I could know Christ personally, experience his resurrection power, be a partner in his suffering, and go all the way with him to death itself. If there was any way to get in on the resurrection from the dead, I wanted to do it (Philippians 3:7-11 MSG).

FIRST WITH CHRIST

Though the first followers of Jesus asked Jesus, *"Where do you live?"* it is a question we need to ask ourselves. *"Where do I live?"* When Jesus called His first group of disciples, He set forth a clear order and priority of their calling.

And He went up on the mountain and summoned those whom He Himself wanted, and they came to

*Him. And He appointed twelve, so that **they would be with Him** and that He could **send them out to preach**, and to **have authority** to cast out the demons* (Mark 3:13-15).

Jesus' first priority was that disciples are first *"with Him."* "Withnessing" comes before witnessing in the priority of Jesus for His disciples. Teaching and especially preaching should be the product of first being with Jesus. If I am not first with Him then I have little to say that is going to change anything—little anointing with which to heal. When I speak the truth which comes from living in the personal presence of Jesus, then I have authority to unseat the entire demonic realm. The order is living in the personal *presence* of Christ and then *preaching* His person, which results in *power*.

Where we live determines what we will become. We are called to live closely with Christ—to be transformed into what and who He is. Maybe this is a foreign or unrealistic thought to you. How can we live close to someone we cannot see? How do we get beyond the superficial acknowledgment of Christ and move into intimacy?

Does it surprise us to know that God is interested in something more than pointing out our flaws and imperfections? God is interested in our holiness, not in a religious regulatory way, but because we live close to Him. If I'm asking where He lives and living there with Him in that moment, then I will become holy.

When God issued an invitation to Moses by igniting a shrub with His presence, Moses left his own course and went into the presence of God. He took off his shoes so as not to track the world into the Presence (see Exod. 3-4). It was not what Moses did that made him holy, but where he lived. To be holy is simply to be devoted to the Lord, to follow Him in everything first, to live a life connected to Him. God is interested in having all of life with us from the deep to the ordinary. He created all the ordinary things.

Often we are like 7th graders at our first dance, hands in our pockets, standing along the wall and staring at the floor, unsure how to make the first move. The truth is God has always made the first move. Jesus walks up to you now and extends His hand to take yours. He not only wants to dance over you,[8] He wants to dance with you. He wants to walk with you—wants you to rest against Him and allow Him to lead the dance.

Where does Jesus live? Where are you and I living?

JOIN *the* JOURNEY

*Jesus turned, saw them following Him, and asked, "What are you looking for?" They answered, "**Where do You live**, Rabbi?" (This word means "Teacher")* (John 1:38 TEV).

Where do you live? The question those first followers asked of Jesus is a question I ask myself. Where do I live? I will know where I live by what I am becoming. Do I smell more like the world or more like Christ?

As you read this Scripture aloud, allow yourself to see it with the eyes of your heart. Put yourself in the place of those first two followers of Jesus. Now, as you stand face-to-face with Christ, He asks you the same question: "Beloved, where are you living?" What are you living for? How would you answer Him? Write down anything the Lord reveals to you as you meditate on this question.

*Where do **you** live?* Reflect on these questions and make a few notes.

1. *What are you becoming?* (Not what have you accomplished.) What has changed in you over the past five years in the way you see other people? How about in your job or career? Your ministry to other people?

_____

_____

_____

_____

2. *What are you feeding in your life?* What kinds of music or teaching do you listen to? What books have you read over the past year?

_____

_____

_____

_____

3. *What does this Scripture mean to you?* Read it a few times aloud; then close your eyes and meditate on it. Then write a few notes after the Scripture.

_____

_____

_____

_____

*But we all, with unveiled face, **beholding** as in a mirror the glory of the Lord, are being **transformed** [becoming] into the same image from glory to glory, just as from the Lord, the Spirit* (2 Corinthians 3:18).

ENDNOTES

1. "Let your house be a gathering place for sages. And wallow in the dust of their feet. And drink in their words with gusto." Jacob Nuesner, *The Mishna: A New Translation* (New Haven and London: Yale University Press, 1998), 673, reference Abot 1:41, B.

2. David Stern describes the relationship between teacher and disciple. "The essence of the relationship was one of trust in every area of living, and its goal was to make the *talmidim* (disciple/becomer) like his rabbi in knowledge, wisdom and ethical behavior." David H. Stern, *Jewish New Testament*

Commentary (Clarksville, MD: Jewish New Testament Publications, 1992), 23.

3. Thomas á Kempis, *The Imitation of Christ: A Contemporary Version,* William Griffin (San Francisco: Harper, 2000).

4. Oswald Chambers, *My Utmost for His Highest* (Grand Rapids MI: Discovery House Publishers, 1992).

5. The Hebrew word for pursuit here is *radaph* (which is to pursue something or someone almost as in hounding them for it).

6. Kempis.

7. The Hebrew word for holy, *qadosh*, describes something or someone set apart and owned by God.

8. Zephaniah 3:17 says God is a victorious and confident Warrior who will rejoice over us. The word translated as "rejoice" refers to a whirling dance of celebration. He dances over and around us.

CHAPTER THREE

THE REST OF THE REST

...They said to Him, "Rabbi (which translated means Teacher), where are You staying?" [Where do you live?] *He said to them, **"Come, and you will see..."*** (John 1:38-39).

THE JOURNEY

Now Jesus set out for home, and we joined Him on the journey, talking along the way. Jesus slowed His pace and waited for us to come alongside Him. As the conversation continued, He asked about us—who we were and where we were from—about our families and how we became followers of John. He talked to us about John to see if we understood the teaching about the coming Messiah. We tossed words back and forth across the road for some period of time. For the most part, there were no deep words or probing questions, just talk. He was interested—He listened. All the while Jesus' steps were certain and deliberate, as if each was a precious possession—something to be savored. He knew where we were going and led the way.

As we neared the place where Jesus lived, we slowed down and approached the door of a humble dwelling no different from the houses around it. As we stood at the door, Jesus extended His callused hand, bending down and slightly forward at the door in a gesture of invitation. Looking inside we could see that His home was simple—not pretentious, but warm and inviting.

Jesus stepped through the door and opened His home to us. There were no waiting servants—no other people or attendants, just the three of us. It was as if the house was expecting us. As our eyes adjusted to the light, we saw a few small clay oil lamps providing a gentle, flickering light. In that warm light was revealed a single piece of furniture: a simple table. It was made from the dark smooth wood of an olive tree. The table was set with a few round loaves of barley bread and a vessel filled with wine. Jesus said, "I made this table with My own hands for just this purpose. Come—come and rest with Me."

COME AND SEE WHAT?

When Jesus invited those first two followers to, *"Come and see,"* He was repeating an invitation flowing from His heart from before time. It is an intimate and transforming invitation to participate in His life—to share in a new quality of life—an abundant, overflowing, overcoming kind of life.

Jesus invited His first two disciples to the home where He was staying on the Sabbath. The text says it was about the 10th hour when the invitation took place. This would be a time when they were to get ready for the Sabbath.[1] The Sabbath is all about *rest*.

Because it was the Sabbath, the two men could not bring any food along or carry any tools. Since the Sabbath began at the end of the day, they knew that Jesus' invitation was for them to come and spend the night wherever He was going. They were going to have to trust that all they needed was going to be found in the rest they would spend with Him.

Jesus' invitation to *"come and see"* was tied to the question, *"What do you seek?"* Jesus knew the answer even as He asked the question. They and we are seeking connection to the One who kissed us alive—the One in whom we live and move and exist—the One who longs to settle down and make His home in our hearts. The thing we are seeking that cannot be found outside of Christ is *rest*.

THE REST OF THE REST

What is rest? For one, rest is a break or a pause. Rest is more than taking a nap, though naps are nice. It is the position we live from. In rest we lean against another and rely upon His strength. As we lean and rest, we are refreshed and regain strength. Rest is stillness in which we recharge and replace what is exhausted in us.

For the most part we have forgotten how to rest. Scripture tells us *"There remains a Sabbath rest for the people of God"* (Heb. 4:9). I might translate it "We have left behind the rest of the rest." It was true two thousand years ago, and it's still true today. There is a rest that we have yet to enter into.

We are a rest-less and disconnected society. A recent survey showed that the average American moves 14 times during his or her lifetime.[2] Amazing! We are unsettled about everything. We have more media and modes of communication than ever, yet we remain disconnected. I recall sitting in the living room with my wife and one of our daughters when all three of us were talking on cell phones and not to each other. We are a restless, unsettled, and disconnected people.

And we *work* very hard at resting, especially in the west. We work *to* rest. Most of us work 50 weeks each year to take two weeks of vacation. We work to save for retirement—to rest at the end of our lives when life has worn us out and put us on the shelf. Rather than working *to* rest, the invitation of Jesus, if we accept it, allows us to work *from* rest.

Rest is not necessarily the absence of work. Jesus indicated that the Father is still working (see John 5:17). Jesus riled up the religious folks by healing on the Sabbath seven times in the Gospels. He said that He was not doing any work, but only focusing on what the Father was doing and then doing likewise (see John 5:19). Whatever Jesus did was from this place of restful focus on the Father—a position of purposeful intimacy.

Rest brings a quietness of heart coming from an awareness of who we are and who God is.[3] When we rest we don't have to put on a religious performance. We can live like we have nothing to prove. Rest carries with it the idea of completion—that there is nothing left to be done. It is finished!

The invitation from Jesus to *come and see* still lingers for us. It is as fresh today as it was the first time He spoke it. He is inviting us to rest. The rest into which Jesus invites us has three facets: Rest *for* God, rest *in* God, and rest received *from* God.[4] First we rest *for* connection with God; then in that connection we find rest *in* the heart of God with the result that He gives us rest *from* all external distraction to live in intimacy with Him.

All three of these facets are part of the invitation from Christ. Rest is then something we *choose,* something we *experience,* and something we *receive.*

REST *FOR* GOD—A CHOICE FOR CONNECTION

The first purpose for rest is connection with God. The Hebrew word we translate "Sabbath" means to cease from work and activity. It is a rest we choose *for* connection with the Father's heart. The Sabbath rest is a pause—a purposeful interlude for intimacy.[5]

God entered the Sabbath rest after creation. When He finished speaking and breathing worlds into being, He stepped back as an artist might do upon completing a masterpiece and said, *"This is good!"*[6] He paused to connect with His creation and instituted the Sabbath rest.

When I think of Sabbath rest, I think of my grandson Tommy who is 3 years old at this writing and is very good at being 3. He runs around with great fury and activity, touching and playing with anything he can reach. Recently he was at our home climbing everything in sight, running around after the dog, and playing with little trucks while making truck noises. (Somehow little boys are programmed to make truck sounds.) After a little while his batteries ran down and he got tired. He grabbed his blanket and his "sippy" and climbed up onto the sofa next to Pap Pap (me). He put his little summer-buzzed head on my lap and settled in. I rubbed his head telling him, "You feel like a little coconut." Tommy just fell asleep for an hour on my lap. That was rest for Tommy and for me—a connection I will treasure forever.

Rest is a pause to step back and look at the perfect beauty of the Lord with awe and wonder. This connection was in the heart of David when he wrote Psalm 27.

> *One thing I have asked from the Lord, that I shall seek: That I may dwell in the house of the Lord all the days of my life, to behold the beauty of the Lord and to meditate in His temple* (Psalm 27:4).

The Sabbath rest is the intentional seeking of His face—the one and only desperate pursuit of our hearts (see Ps. 27:8). When David said he desired to *"meditate in His temple,"* he was deliberately choosing to fill his eyes and heart with thoughts and images of Yahweh as the highest priority of his life. David sought the presence of God as a precious treasure—as the only thing worth having.[7] In that seeking, we connect with the deep places in the mystery of God. Job declares, *"How great is God—beyond our understanding..."* (Job 36:26 NIV).

Recently Carol and I took advantage of a historic tour of Savannah, Georgia. The tour director recommended that we stop to see the Cathedral of St. John the Baptist. I've seen cathedrals all over the world and was not especially excited to see another one, but we stopped anyway. We swam through the near 100-degree heat and humidity to the open door of the cathedral. I was unprepared for what I would see as we stepped into the rear of the church. I literally gasped. My eyes were filled and overwhelmed with the ornate beauty and quiet solemnity of this cathedral. Refracted, variegated light streamed through dozens of brilliant stained glass windows which illuminated the gold ornamentation and walls covered with pictures of biblical stories. There was a golden throne positioned in the front of the cathedral, beyond the altar, surrounded by marble and gold. The prismatic effect of the stained glass seemed to break down the streaming sunlight to display the glory of Heavens' vault. I felt as though I had stepped into the very throne room of Heaven.

I was arrested by the beauty of God. The majesty and holiness of God took me into custody. A sweet little nun came up to me while I was entranced and quietly asked me to remove the baseball cap which protected my bare head from the hot sun. I wanted to sit down in that place to consider the beauty of the Godhead. I was filled with joy and longing at the same time. As Carol and I walked out, my eyes filled with tears and I muttered, "We've lost the awe... we've lost the awe."

We have lost the mystery of meditating on God—the awe of God's presence—the take-your-breath-away gasp of beholding His glory. We have Him all figured out. In the Sabbath rest, we behold the Lord and find a transforming intimacy. In our humanness we are afraid of this transforming intimacy—that there might be something outside our understanding and control—something we don't have figured out. As we rest for connection with the Eternal, we also find connection with one another. We are set apart for Christ and the Christ we find in one another.

As we rest for connection with the Eternal, we become more like Him. Paul said:

> *Now, the Lord is the Spirit, and wherever the Spirit of the Lord is, He gives freedom. And all of us have had that veil removed so that we can be mirrors that brightly reflect the glory of the Lord. And as the Spirit of the Lord works within us,* **we become more and more like Him and reflect His glory even more** (2 Corinthians 3:17-18 NLT).

Sabbath is more than a set of religious restrictions. In the New Covenant we do not keep the Sabbath; the Sabbath keeps us. Jesus brought those first two "becomers" to His house to model Sabbath rest—to make a connection with them. There had to be a coming away—a moving in with Rest Himself.

REST *IN* GOD—A REST WE EXPERIENCE

Have you ever been awakened on a spring or summer morning when it was raining outside? The sound of the raindrops hitting the roof is hypnotic—it's like a drug that makes you want to roll over and go back to sleep. It's a sound that says, "There is nothing more important that you have to do today than stay in this bed." Then, when you've become more fully awakened, your mind fills with the stuff you have to do that day. The list grows and your rest gives way to reality and routine. What would it feel like to know that you really could just roll over and go back to sleep—to have your heart and busy mind convinced by the steady beating and white noise of rain hitting the roof above you that there is nothing more important awaiting you?

There is a rolling over kind of rest that comes with feelings of calm and settledness. It is the rest *in* God. This rest comes from the same Hebrew word from which the biblical Noah's name is derived. Noah rested in the ark, where the only thing to listen to was the sound of the water outside the ark. This is the kind of rest an unborn child could experience in the mother's womb. The thing the child is aware of is the sound of the fluid in the womb and little else. All of the child's needs are met in the mother just as all of the needs of Noah and his family were met in the ark.

When we rest in God we have the intimate sense of His personal presence. We talked first about the rest *for* God, where we focus on His face, and that then leads to our rest *in* God, where we are cocooned in the embrace of the Father's love toward us.

When our kids were very young, they saw their Daddy sitting with stacks of books and papers piled on the living room couch and end tables. My most common resource was an old single column Bible held together in a brown leather case; through it I came to a desperate pursuit of God.

One morning our family heard that a little girl about the same age as our daughter Christina, (Coco in real life) had been hit and killed by a school bus. This was a great shock to us all, but especially to Coco, who was about six years old at the time. I guess it had not entered her mind that a little child could die. She was scared. We didn't talk much that day about what had happened.

Later that evening we put the girls to bed, praying over them as we often did. After the kids were settled, I returned to the living room of our little ranch home and sat down, surrounded by books and note pads. Suddenly I realized I couldn't find my Bible. I looked all over the house, thinking I had set it down in some strange place. As a last resort I looked in the kid's rooms. When I came to Coco's room, I found that she had taken Daddy's Bible and was sleeping with it under her pillow. I guess she figured that if this old Bible made Daddy safe, then it would do the same for her. She rested in what Daddy rested in.

There is a rest for us to experience *in* Christ. It is a rest that comes from and leads to intimacy. Christ is the model for this rest.

> *Do you believe that **I am in the Father, and the Father is in Me**? The words that I say to you I do not speak on My own initiative, but the Father **abiding in Me** does His works. Believe Me that I am in the Father and the Father **is** in Me; otherwise believe because of the works themselves* (John 14:10-11).

When Jesus said that He is *in* the Father and the Father is *in* Him, He was saying that they *rest* in one another.[8] Jesus also invited us to abide or rest in Him, and He promised to abide in us and to birth fruit in us through that abiding relationship.

> *Abide in Me, and I in you. As the branch cannot bear fruit of itself unless it abides in the vine, so neither can you unless you **abide** in Me. I am the vine, you are the branches; he who **abides** in Me and I in him, he bears much fruit, for apart from Me you can do nothing. If anyone does not **abide** in Me, he is thrown away as a branch and dries up; and they gather them, and cast them into the fire and they are burned. If you **abide** in Me, and My words **abide** in you, ask whatever you wish, and it will be done for you. My Father is glorified by this, that you bear much fruit, and so prove to be My disciples* (John 15:4-8).*

Look at the number of times Jesus used the word *abide*. To abide is to rest in, live in, or remain in, to be focused on Christ. Abiding also carries the feeling of expectation.[9] Something is going to be produced as we rest, remain, abide, focus, or seek after personal intimacy with Christ. We plant a seed in the ground, and there is an expectation of life breaking through into the light. I have never planted a seed and waited for grunting noises as something came up through the ground. Life happens from rest.

Paul used the phrase *in Christ* or something very similar more than 25 times in His letter to the Ephesians. That would be a chapter in itself. We are chosen *in* Christ, purposed *in* Christ, have hope *in* Christ, are redeemed and forgiven *in* Christ, made heirs *in* Christ, become alive *in* Christ, are seated *in* Christ, and many more. All of these are aspects of resting *in* Christ.

As we rest *in* Christ, we bear the fruit He produces. We can rest knowing that it is not up to us to come up with an answer or fruit. The fruit is the character of Christ. We bear it—we display it. As we rest in Christ, His word and heart abide in us; we glorify the Father; we bear much fruit from the seed of His life in us and give proof that we are becoming who He is.

REST RECEIVED *FROM* GOD—A REST GOD GIVES

As we rest *for* connection with Christ, we come to a place of resting *in* Christ. As we rest *in* Christ, He gives us rest *from* striving and struggle.[10] We come to a place of quiet where we can *"cease striving and know that* [He is] *God"* (Ps. 46:10).

> *For thus the Lord God, the Holy One of Israel, has said, "In repentance and rest* [nuach, rest in God] *you will be saved, in quietness* [shaqat, rest from God] *and trust is your strength..."* (Isaiah 30:15).

Our ultimate rest is in the very nature of God. With rest God imparts security. We are as secure as an unborn child in the mother's womb; all that we need flows to us from His compassion in intimate quietness. The main purpose of the rest we receive from God is to know Him. *"This is eternal life, that they may know You..."* (John 17:3). As we find rest, we stop squirming in the lap of the Father and live in the fruit of Christ's victory over sin and death.

How do we know when we've entered into this rest that remains for us? When I'm at rest, I live like I have nothing to prove. My life ceases to be a performance and I am quieter. Jesus is the perfect model of one who has entered into rest. His life was one of total connection—total rest in the Father. As Jesus rested in the Father, He was able to withstand even the cross. The result of Jesus resting in the Father was a union with Him—the same union that is available to us.

The goal of all that Christ did was to bring us to the place of quietness and rest to hear His voice. Jesus said,

> *My sheep recognize My voice. I know them, and they follow Me. I give them real and eternal life. They are protected from the Destroyer for good. No one can steal them from out of My hand* (John 10:27-28 MSG).

We cannot recognize the voice of the Shepherd if we are busy listening to all of the voices around us. The goal of rest—the goal of the Gospel—is to bring us to the place of intimate quiet so that we can hear Him and respond to His invitation. It is an invitation that comes from His residence within us.

> *The goal is for all of them to become one heart and mind— just as You, Father, are in Me and I in You, so they might be one heart and mind with us. Then the world might believe that You, in fact, sent Me. The same glory You gave Me, I gave them, so they'll be as unified and together as We are—I in them and You in Me. Then they'll be mature in this oneness, and give the godless world evidence that You've sent Me and loved them in the same way You've loved Me* (John 17:21-23 MSG).

Oswald Chambers connects rest with becoming one with God. He says that resting *in* God and the rest we receive *from* God "means a total oneness with Him. And this oneness will make us not only blameless in His sight, but also a profound joy to Him."[11]

When Jesus invited those brothers and us to "come and see" where He lived, He was inviting us to rest—to become one with Him. We are invited to come aside and to put down the stuff of life we carry around that robs and distracts us with its clanking preoccupations.

Jesus invites us to a rest *for* Him, for the purpose of connection with Him; a rest *in* Him, which transforms us to become like Him; and a rest received *from* Him, bringing us to a place of quiet oneness with Him. Jesus invites us:

> **Come to Me**, *all who are weary and heavy-laden, and I will give you rest. Take My yoke upon you and learn from Me, for I am gentle and humble in heart, and* **you will find rest for your souls**. *For My yoke is easy and My burden is light* (Matthew 11:28-30).

A great emblem of Christ's invitation is the table. At the table we connect with Him, focused on His face as though we only have eyes for Him. At the table we cease wiggling and settle into our chairs to become like Him. At the table the world grows dim to us and Christ becomes our universe—His heartbeat becomes the rhythm of our lives. When we have arrived at His table, we have arrived at our destiny. His table is the forum of His intimate intentions from the beginning of time until time is folded up and put away.

Come and See...

JOIN *the* JOURNEY

> **Come to Me**, *all who are weary and heavy-laden, and I will give you rest. Take My yoke upon you and learn from Me, for I am gentle and humble in heart, and **you will find rest for your souls**. For My yoke is easy and My burden is light* (Matthew 11:28-30).

Quiet yourself and read the above Scripture a few times aloud; then close your eyes and meditate on it. What kinds of images come to your heart as you meditate? What do you sense Jesus communicating to your heart as you come to Him?

_____

_____

_____

_____

_____

_____

Rest is the inner quiet that comes from intimacy with Christ. For us to experience this rest, we must learn to release the things that make us weary and load us down. As you are in the presence of Jesus, ask Him to bring to your heart the things that rob you of rest.

Here are a few practical questions that might help you to identify what robs you of rest.

1. Where do you see yourself as indispensible in your life, family, or career?

   _____

   _____

   _____

   _____

   _____

   _____

2. How and when do you take a personal Sabbath to connect with the heart of God? What tries to keep you from it?

   _____

   _____

   _____

   _____

   _____

   _____

ENDNOTES

1. According to the Talmud, there were only certain days on which a wedding could normally take place so as not to interfere with Shabbat. By counting backward from the wedding feast of Cana (recorded in John 2) we arrive at Shabbat.

2. Karen Bogenschneider, "Family Policy Matters, How Policy Making Affects Families and What Professionals Can Do," (Mahwah, NJ: Lawrence Erlbaum Assoc, Inc., 2002).

3. Dr. Siang-Yang Tan describes what rest looks like in his book *Rest, Experiencing God's Peace in a Restless World* (Ann Arbor, MI: Servant Publications, 2000).

4. There are three Hebrew words that are often translated as rest, *shabbat, nuach,* and *shaqat,* which occur in an unfolding order throughout the Bible. I first rest to connect with the heart of God, which leads to a resting in him ultimately allowing us to receive rest from God for all the distractions in the world.

5. The Greek word most often translated as "rest" is *anapausis,* used here, from which we get our English word, *pause.* It is an interlude as if between movements of a musical piece.

6. The Hebrew translated "ended" is the word *kalah,* which carries the idea of something completed, but also a sense of longing.

7. The Hebrew word translated as "meditate" here is the word *baqar,* which represents seeking as highest priority. This same root is used in the word *morning,* as in before anything else.

8. The Greek preposition translated "in" is *en,* which holds the sense of abiding or resting in relationship.

9. The Greek word translated "abide" is *meno,* which connects two persons or objects together. There is the feeling that something will be born from the connection, adding expectancy.

10. This rest stems from the word *shaqat,* meaning tranquility or rest from inner anxiety and external circumstances. It is sometimes translated as "quietness" (see Isa. 30:15) or "settled" (see Jer. 48:11). *Shaqat* carries with it the sense of security and is sometimes used alongside *shalom*, which is used in giving rest from war and the enemy (see Josh. 11:23).

11. Oswald Chambers, *My Utmost for His Highest* (Grand Rapids, MI: Discovery House Publishers, 1992).

Chapter Four

The Longing

As we came to the door where Jesus was staying, Jesus stepped inside and opened His home to us. There was a fire already kindled and a few small oil lamps providing a gentle light. Emerging from the flicker of that soft light was a single piece of furniture in the room: a simple table. It was made from the wood of an olive tree, dark and rich. The table was humble in shape and design, showing simple but excellent workmanship. The loving hands of the Carpenter had been over this from rough cut planks to the smooth finish. Our eyes were drawn to the table that invited us to come and rest, not with a word, but by its very presence. Jesus gave voice to the mute invitation of the table, saying, "I made this table just for you—for just this purpose. I've brought you here to rest with me at the table."

As we entered the room there was a small stool just inside the door. Jesus invited us, one then the other, to sit on the stool. We had walked some distance and our feet were covered with the dust of the day. Our feet had to be washed. This was usually the task of the lowest servant. But Jesus, the Lamb, was going to wash our feet! It was all out of place. Who was this Lamb—this One whom John recommended to us?

I settled onto the stool and Jesus untied my sandals and put them aside. He got up and walked away for a moment, returning with a basin of clean water. Wrapping a towel around his waist, Jesus knelt at my feet and looked up into my eyes to determine whether I was willing to place my feet in the earthen basin. I was reluctant. How could this be proper to allow Jesus, the One whom John had waited for, to serve us in the most menial way? I should have washed His feet. Then He said, "I did not come to be served, but to serve and give." I cautiously nodded my head to Jesus, who looked up at me and began to pour water on my feet. As the water coursed over my feet, I thought of the long journey—not just the journey that day, but of all the previous days when we had left home and followed John. With each application of water, the dust and debris of the journey was being washed away, preparing me for the present moment with Jesus, the Lamb. As the dust was removed, I became aware of the immediate moment with my feet in the basin in the hands of Jesus.

Jesus took the towel and dried my feet. I stood up, turned toward the center of the room, and saw the simple table before me. Jesus walked around to the other side of the table and spread out His hands in a gesture of invitation to us—to me. I felt at once an excitement and longing, as if there was a place prepared just for me, that without me at the table something would be out of place. I focused on the table and felt the heaviness of life that I had carried into that house. Everything inside me, questions, distractions, weariness, was drawn toward that simple table—the realm of rest and connection. Jesus said only a word, "Come!"

Before the beginning—before there was anything, there was Love: a desperate longing in search of a home.[1] This longing Love was more than a feeling or a noble thought; it was the inspiration which breathed a universe into being from snails to supernovas. God is a connecting, covenant God who lives in community within Himself. His nature is the very definition of intimacy filled with joy, dancing, celebration, and boundless creativity.[2]

The Scripture says, *"God is love"* (see 1 John 4:8,16). God, within Himself, is both source and object of selfless giving and sharing. John, the beloved disciple of Jesus, declared that God is not only Love, but also that *"God is light and in Him there is no darkness at all"* (1 John 1:5). If we translated this verse back into Hebrew, we would have an expanded perspective of the community of God. It would read *"Elohiym* [plural, indicating three] *is light and among those three there is no kind of darkness at all."* There is no darkness or misunderstanding. There is total transparency, complete communion with total unity of purpose and being. God, within Himself, is totally *present* to Himself.

Brennan Manning, who refers to God as the "originating lover," discusses the longing love of God.

The foundation of the furious longing of God is the Father who is the originating Lover, the Son who is the full self-expression of that Love, and the Spirit who is the original and inexhaustible activity of that Love, drawing the created universe into itself.[3]

This furious longing of God is portrayed many different ways in the Scriptures. It is the longing of the aged father for the lost son in Luke 15. It is the longing for the bride by the heroic king in the Song of Songs. It is the constant declaration of Yahweh to lead His people Israel into the land of promise so that He would be their God; they would be His people and He would live among them. It is the plaintive lament of Jesus outside the walls of Jerusalem; *"How often I wanted to gather you to Myself, but you would not come"* (see Luke 13:34).

Father, Son, and Spirit reach outside themselves to draw us into intimate presence. We become the objects of this longing, sharing love—part of the celebration. God draws us to into the circle of His intimate love and loves us with the same intensity with which He loves Himself. And my heart finds a deep and personal rest when I realize that the Father loves me with the same intensity with which He loves the Son.

> *The glory which You have given Me I have given to*
> *them, that they may be one, just as We are one; I in*
> *them and You in Me, that they may be perfected in*
> *unity, so that the world may know that You sent Me,*

and loved them, even as You have loved Me (John
17:22-23).

An image that occurs throughout Scripture that represents this
kind of intimate connection, the longing love of God Himself, is the
table.[4] The table represents provision, grace, community, belonging,
mutual acceptance, and giving. More than anything else, the table
represents a face-to-face connection with the Eternal. It is the very
picture of true intimacy and the platform of longing love. With this
intimacy comes rest. It is the same restful, purposeful intimacy with
which John rested against the breast of Jesus at the table. It is a rest
of acute awareness and connection with the heart of Christ. From
the very beginning, it has been the intention of Heaven to draw us
back to the table we abandoned in Eden. All that the Lord has done
has been with the purpose of bringing us to the table, which is to say
into His intimate circle of love.

THE CONVERSATION CONTINUES

The longing that Jesus touched on in that first conversation
with His disciples on the road to His house actually comes from the
longing in God's heart. It is the conversation within the very heart
of the Eternal. We long for Him because, and only because, He first
longed for us. *"We love, because He first loved us"* (1 John 4:19).
Jesus' first words to us, *"What are you looking for?"* tell us there is
a constant and ongoing longing to reconnect with the heart and
love of God that was lost in Eden. It does not originate in us, but it
echoes back from the Father's longing heart through us.

God is not interested in more religion or better ways to experience miracles. Sacrifice and offerings are not what He wants. What He wants—what He longs for—are broken and humble hearts. The humble heart is not one filled with rules and mere religious proscriptions; it is the heart that knows it is welcomed to the King's table. Listen to the Psalms and the Prophets.

> *Going through the motions doesn't please You, a flawless performance is nothing to You. I learned God-worship when my pride was shattered. Heart-shattered lives ready for love don't for a moment escape God's notice* (Psalm 51:16-17 MSG).

> *I'm after love that lasts, not more religion. I want you to know God, not go to more prayer meetings* (Hosea 6:6 MSG).

God is not interested in another flawless performance; He has already done that. He is after "God-worship," not self-absorbed performance religion that ranges from the most formal to the most charismatic expressions of church and also includes secular humanism.

Let's clear up the term *religion* for a moment. I've gotten in trouble with folks from the more formal church traditions and Catholicism. Religion is, or at least should be, the practice or expression of the condition of a heart connected and in love with Christ personally. It is not always so. Sometimes religion becomes a form that has no connection or transformational property in God. It is a tradition or ceremony we go through to alleviate spiritual obligation without regarding the one to whom we are obliged. In the time of the

Old Testament saints, there were times when the form overtook the substance.

Jesus was irritated about people going through religious motions with no connection to God. In one case, religious types deprived their own parents of what they needed in order to observe a tradition that was more about how they wanted people to see them than reflecting the heart and mercy upon which the Law rested. They robbed God—they robbed man—they robbed their own families! They missed the point of tithing, which is about lordship and trust, not about prosperity and legalism to impress each other (see Matt. 15:1-9). They pretended to follow the Law, but actually missed it by a mile by not giving to their own families. Jesus called them hypocrites—gamers. He told them they were blind guides, not seeing the point of the Law. They wore the false face of piety and religion and their parents starved. That is what I mean by religion. Jesus went on to say that they talked a good talk, but their hearts were far away from Him.

God's kind of religion has little to do with practice and formality and much more to do with expressing His heart of compassion. The Epistle of James describes *"pure and undefiled religion"* as caring for the poor widows and orphans and otherwise helpless people around us. In other words, true or pure religion expresses the heart and nature of God (see James 1:27).

THE GOD WHO GATHERS

As we said in an earlier chapter, the things we seek after tend to determine how we spend our lives and resources. It is no different with God, the original longing lover. In fact, God spent everything—became one of us in His loving pursuit. He is a seeker without peer—one who seeks worshipers in Spirit and truth (see John 4:23).

God held nothing back in His pursuit. Though it seems cliché to us now, the Scripture is true, "God *so* loved the world that He dismembered Himself, giving His only begotten Son, that whoever believed Him and His invitation would not die in despair away from His table and presence, but would experience eternal life—the same kind of life God Himself lives" (John 3:16 author's paraphrase). The word that stands out to me there is *so*, expressing the ache of the longing love of God to bring us back to the table abandoned at Eden.

Beloved, God is a gatherer—one who created us with dust and the condensation of His own breath, one who longs to bring us to His table. Christ has done all to bring us to the table so that He might love us there, even including washing our feet. Otherwise we are distracted from Him. As we will talk about later, we are sometimes not really *present* to God or each other (for that matter). Because of our distraction with the world, we seldom experience true spiritual intimacy, which is the conduit of this longing love of God. True intimacy exists where we become open and available to God or each other, where there is mutual vulnerability which leads to transformation.

The very essence of love is giving—giving to another. God is totally love; God is totally giving. In that giving love Christ has washed our feet to bring us to the table. We could not come into His house and to His table tracking in the dust and debris of the world. To be sure, it would be a humbling thought for any of us that

Jesus would wash our feet as He did with His first intimate followers prior to His crucifixion. Peter did not respond well, nor did he understand why Jesus would perform such a servile act. When Jesus invited Peter to put his feet in the basin, there was an eruption of pride in Peter's heart. He defied Jesus! *"No," Peter protested, "You will never ever wash my feet!" Jesus replied, "Unless I wash you, you won't belong to Me"* (John 13:8 NLT). What?! *"No?!"*

Jesus washed the feet of His followers to prepare them to receive the Kingdom of God. Jesus had to do this before His arrest and execution or they would spend all of their time shuffling for position. They had to belong totally to Jesus. Jesus is washing away anything that keeps us from His table, such as worry, delay, distraction, or disappointments of the day. To worry is to be taken in two directions at the same time.

Worry chokes and suffocates spiritual life—all life.

> ...***Worry*** *of the world and the deceitfulness of wealth* ***choke the word****, and it becomes* ***unfruitful*** (Matthew 13:22).

> *Be on guard, so that your hearts will not be* ***weighted down*** *with* ***dissipation*** *and* ***drunkenness*** *and the* ***worries of life****, and that day will not come on you suddenly like a* ***trap*** (Luke 21:34).

Worry chokes us, weighs us down. Try dancing with a ball and chain around your ankles. It causes us to stagger and stumble like men drunk and disoriented. Worry mugs us on the outskirts of God's best and traps us into a life away from intimacy.

I recall with sadness a time when our kids were very young and we, actually I, was still in the retail music business. I say that I was in the music business because, in fact, I never allowed my wife Carol inside of all that was happening. It was in the summertime and we all needed a break. I called and reserved a place where we were going to stay in Chincoteague, and we packed the minivan and were ready to go.

Before I left the driveway, I just had to look at the mail. When I did, I found some kind of bad financial news, the nature of which I do not specifically recall at the moment. I was filled with worry and anger at the same time and declared, "We cannot go on this vacation!" We unpacked the van and never went because of worry. I wounded my wife and my children that day, and worry robbed us and caused me to stagger like a drunken man out of my mind.

It has been many years now since that day. I would give any-thing to have that time back which I forfeited to worry. I would have loved to be on the beach with my two precious girls and play in the sand and surf. I long for it.

Beloved, the Lord longs for us to know Him, to experience His *peace,* His *power,* and His *presence.* And we will experience these as our longing agrees with the longing of the Lord's heart.

> *Therefore the Lord **longs** to be gracious to you, and therefore He waits on high to have compassion on you. For the Lord is a God of justice; how blessed are all those who **long** for Him* (Isaiah 30:18).

John observed that Jesus loved His followers to the end (see John 13:1); He held nothing back. His objective was intimacy. If we are to enter that kind of relationship, then we too must hold nothing back. There can be no obstacles between our faces and the face of Christ at His table. All of this was so that we could come back to the same position we held when we drew our first breath: *face-to-face*.

JOIN *the* JOURNEY

> *Therefore the Lord **longs** to be gracious to you, and therefore He waits on high to have compassion on you. For the Lord is a God of justice; how blessed are all those who **long** for Him* (Isaiah 30:18).

Take a few minutes and read this verse aloud to yourself. What words or thoughts or images stand out to you as you meditate on the verse? Take a few minutes and write them down here.

_____

_____

_____

What kinds of things distract your attention from the Lord and people? Consider the last time you were in a place of meditation or devotion with the Lord. What else seemed important to you while you were in this time? Let's bring it further down to earth. What gets in the way when you are with someone else you care deeply about? Are you trying to impress them? Where do your thoughts seem to wander? Write them down here.

_____

_____

_____

What does it mean to you that the Lord longs to be gracious to you? Stop and soak in that thought. Write your thoughts here.

_____

_____

_____

ENDNOTES

1. The Hebrew word translated "love" begins with the letter *aleph* and ends with the letter *beth.* The letter *aleph* represents a longing or aching sound while the letter *beth* represents a house. *Love* could be defined as a longing looking for a home.

2. God's nature is described by the word *perichorisis*, which is literally translated "circle dance."

3. Brennan Manning, *The Furious Longing of God* (Colorado Springs, CO: David C. Cook, 2009).

4 The Hebrew for table in the torah is *shulchan,* which could mean anything from a leather mat to the table of showbread.

CHAPTER FIVE

FACE TO FACE

Thus the Lord used to speak to Moses face to face, just as a man speaks to his friend... (Exodus 33:11).

I have been playing the trumpet as long as I can remember—so long that it's hard for me to recall a time when I didn't. I picked up my older brother's cornet at the age of eight when he joined the Marines, and I taught myself to play. By the time I got to high school, playing the trumpet had become more than a hobby; it was my obsession—my identity. Aside from the school activities, I also played professionally in bands alongside guys who were several years older than me. Playing music was the way I found acceptance and belonging.

During those years I was enthralled with an almost religious veneration by one particular trumpeter, Doc Severinsen. He led the *Tonight Show* band and was just an unbelievable player in every respect. I stayed up late nearly every night to watch the *Johnny Carson Show* just to hear Doc screaming out some high note at the end of a commercial break. Now and then the whole band would play a chart, and I would sit alone in the darkness, interrupted only by the flickering of the black and white television. I was into it. I got hold of every one of his recordings and listened to them over and over again. I wanted to be just like Doc.

In the winter of my senior year, I attended a band concert at the Blackstone in downtown Chicago where Doc Severinsen was the featured trumpet soloist. After the performance, in which Doc played brilliantly, we were standing outside the door of the concert hall. Then, in a surreal moment, the door opened and Doc himself with an entourage of important-looking people walked out and right past us—right past me! I was on trumpet holy ground. He was the god of trumpet, and I was the 18-year-old lump of nothingness standing frozen and mute as he breezed past me. I was in awe.

I got hold of the recording of the performance and listened to it over and over again until I could imitate his performance within mortal limitations. I was so caught up with Doc that I eventually went out and bought a trumpet just like the one he played. I cut my mustache to be just like his. I would practice my trumpet in front of a mirror to perfect the looks and the moves of my hero. All I wanted in life was to play just like Doc. Alas, though I would eventually develop into a competent trumpet player and major in music, I would never be Doc.

Almost 20 years later, I was attending a music industry trade show in Chicago with a friend. This was now several years after coming to faith in Christ, and though I still played the trumpet, it was no longer a religion to me. As we walked through the door to leave the exhibits and the show, we passed a small booth filled with bright and shining silver trumpets. As we approached the booth, my friend Joe Messich said, "Thom, is that who I think it is sitting in the booth? That's Doc Severinsen!" Lo and behold, there was Doc, my hero, sitting at one end of the sofa. He was 20 years older, but for that moment it seemed that neither one of us had aged for those years. I felt again as though I was that 18-year-old glazed trumpet worshiper and he was the god of trumpet. As I walked in his direction, Doc got up and extended his hand to me. It was another unreal moment as he introduced himself, as if I had no idea who he was.

I was trying to look interested in the trumpets and asked him several questions that would indicate that I knew something about trumpets. Doc then asked me, "Do you play?" What?! The Doc just asked me if I played the trumpet. "Yeah, I play a little bit," I said. Then in a moment I will never forget, Doc turned around and went to his own trumpet case and pulled out his trumpet and handed it to me. *To me!!* This was Doc the heck Severinsen who had just handed me his own horn.

Maintaining my cool, I pulled out my own mouthpiece and put it into Doc's trumpet. *Doc's trumpet!!* (I used to carry around my own mouthpiece in a leather pouch in my pocket. You never know when someone is going to walk up to you and ask you to play a trumpet.) Then I began to play a little melody from a Charlier etude. To my surprise, the sound was warm and lyrical, not nervous. As I played I was less aware of Doc Severinsen standing beside me. I just played the music. As I finished I saw Doc's face, which had broken into a warm smile. With that, Doc said, "Ahh, a little Charlier." At that moment I was aware that it was no longer the hero and the kid standing there; it was just two trumpet players *face-to-face* listening to the music. It was not about *me*. Doc was not adjudicating my performance. He knew who he was. He could have crushed me, this hero of mine. But he just listened to the music. Come on, I'm no Doc. But in fairness, neither is he Thom Gardner. We were just two people listening to the music. With that, we talked about trumpets for a few minutes and my friend took my picture with Doc Severinsen before we left the show. I will never forget the moment. It was not about me; it was all about the music and a *face-to-face* encounter.

I wonder how many times we have missed the music in our relationship with the Lord—the intimate mingling of His Spirit with ours. There is a love song of incomparable timbre carried in His love for us—a love song of incalculable sweetness and intensity. It's the same song I hear when I look into the faces of my children or when one of my grandkids climbs up into my lap with peanut butter breath. Our Father rejoices over us, and all the while we ignore the strains of His passionate love song (see Zeph. 3:17 NIV). But we have practiced our relationship with the Eternal in a mirror much as I used to practice my trumpet. We have been so concerned about how we look *in* God's eyes that we have failed to look *into* God's eyes. There is too often something like a mirror between our faces and our Father's, and we are the ones who put it there. It seems that the greatest obstacle between my face and the Father's is me!!

THE DIM REFLECTION OF SELF

The apostle Paul wrote, *"For now we see in a mirror dimly..."* (1 Cor. 13:12a). The context is love—the *"more excellent way,"* the *perfection* that comes, causing the imperfect to pass away (see 1 Cor. 13:10). The love Paul talked about is the kind of love that begins in the Father as a condition of His heart. This kind of love eludes us when we fix our eyes on the vague reflection in the mirror of self-righteousness and mere religion. In the days Paul wrote about the mirror, there were no such things as plate glass mirrors. The mirrors were made of hammered metal, usually bronze or brass. The reflections were much distorted at best. We are so busy trying to impress God and ourselves that we ignore Him. *We have missed the music!*

Beloved, we are created to live *face-to-face, presence-to-presence* with our Father. We bear His very breath!! The Eternal kissed us alive, intending that we would never turn away. Yet we so often live in the mirror. When I live in the mirror, I am looking at myself or my past or comparing myself with you. I look at myself trying to improve or impress myself and you. I see what is right or wrong with me and find myself wanting. I become fascinated with the mirror and cannot see you or anyone else. I look at my imperfections—a pimple here and too much scalp there. As I look in the mirror, I age. I no longer see the 20-something young person; I see Elmer Fudd!

When I live in the mirror, I am always looking at my past, and I fail to see the present or the future. I see where I blew it and where there seems to be no hope. I cannot move beyond that deadly offense or believe that the Father would see anything beyond that failure.

When we live in this face-to-face kind of relationship, we are not looking around for the right thing to *do* or trying to impress God with our deep spiritual insights. He knows who He is. We are born to live within a breath's distance of a Father who is passionate about seeing our faces. Imagine the ache in His heart when we turn aside because we have looked in the mirror and seen that our lives are not yet perfect. He sees us perfectly, and He has called us to move beyond the mirror and into His face and presence.

AN OBSTRUCTED FOCUS

God reminded Moses of His priority of living face-to-face in the first of the Ten Commandments. God said, *"I am the Lord your God, who brought you out of the land of Egypt, out of the house of slavery. You shall have no other gods before Me"* (Exod. 20:2-3). A literal rendering of the Hebrew text translated "before Me" suggests something like, "You shall have no strange gods (or anything else for that matter) before My face." The words for *face* and *presence* are substantially the same in Hebrew. It is the heart of God that we would live in an intimate awareness of His presence and heart. This is the place of ultimate power and love.

Brennan Manning said:

The gospel proclaims a hidden power in the world—the living presence of the risen Christ. It liberates men and women from the slavery that obscures in them the image and likeness of God.[1]

Beloved, we have damaged and distorted images of ourselves and the One who calls us to a deep and quenching intimacy.

TWO FACES

When I read these first words of the Ten Commandments, an image of two faces comes to mind: Christ's and mine. And there is a junkyard of debris laying between them on the table. I see this junk between the faces of married people all the time. Marriage is much like two people sitting down at a table across from each other. Two people come together and are in love with each other.

In the beginning they can see one another and are able to love and be loved. But as life happens, a layer of undealt with offenses piles up between them until they can no longer see one another; they are looking at the pile of rubble. Here lies the rusting hulk of failed marriages, the broken remnants of familial relationships. In this no man's land of rubble, there are burnt and broken stones cast aside from past failures and unrealized dreams.

Between Abba and us there is the tangled junk of performance and the many ways we've tried to earn what was already freely ours. Likewise, the Father's passion to see our faces is obstructed with sin, self-effort, and issues growing from the bitter roots of past hurts. This junk cannot be overlooked and shoved aside; it must be hauled out to the curb with the rest of the trash.

There are so many things that have obstructed our focus from our Father's face. When Adam and Eve stumbled in the garden, they removed their focus from the Father's face and put it on themselves. Ever since the fall, we have been fascinated with the mirror and our shortcomings. We have squandered precious face time with God and stood in front of the mirror practicing our religion just as I used to practice my trumpet. We are trying to get all the moves down and look good to the world and God. We are fascinated with ourselves and locked onto our imperfections. Both we and the one who invites us to intimacy are deprived of each other's eyes.

When we spend our lives looking into the mirror, ignoring the eyes of our Father, we reject ourselves. Henri Nouwen said "Over the years, I have come to realize that the greatest trap in our life is self-rejection."[2] We live in a culture of mirrors and self-rejection.

Oh, how we are seduced by the mirror! Even when we have come to experience a saving personal knowledge, we take our eyes off the Father's face and return to the mirror.

> *But now that you have come to know God, or rather to be known by God, how is it that you turn back again to the weak and worthless elemental things, to which you desire to be enslaved all over again?* (Galatians 4:9)

What will ever get our focus off of ourselves and back onto the face of our Father? There is only one way, and that is the way of mercy released in repentance. Repentance, in the Hebraic sense, is simply turning back. But it is not just turning in another futile direction. So many of us keep turning like whirling dervishes to other things to validate or excuse whatever we have seen in the mirror. But we seldom turn back toward His face. How many times did the heart of the Father cry out through the Law and the Prophets, *"Return to Me..."*? Repentance is simply turning back toward the Father's face where we were created to live.

We have lived life in the dim and shadowy reflections of a mirror. *"For **now** we see in a mirror dimly, but **then** face to face; **now** I know in part, but **then** I will know fully just as I also have been fully known"* (1 Cor. 13:12). When is the "then" Paul was talking about? There is a greater knowing of God, face-to-face. It is when the imperfect passes away, when we put aside the mirror and look deeply into the eyes of the one who created us to love Him.

Beloved, our Father has a passion for our faces. He has withheld nothing to remove the obstacles and shadows that have come between us—to remove the mirror and call us back to His face. It is only when we look into His face that we will know our Father's heart and our truest selves. The Psalmist said, *"They looked to Him and were radiant, and their faces will never be ashamed"* (Ps. 34:5).

When we take our eyes off of the mirror and again *"look to Him"* we become *"radiant;"* we literally sparkle in His presence. We no longer focus on ourselves, our past wounds, our offenses, or our sins. We are now focused again on the Lord for whom we were created and recreated in Christ Jesus. The Father has removed every obstacle in Christ Jesus, according to His great love toward us, as expressed in mercy.

> *They will see His face, and His name will be on their foreheads* (Revelation 22:4).

JOIN *the* JOURNEY

Thus the Lord used to speak to Moses face to face, just
as a man speaks to his friend... (Exodus 33:11).

What an amazing picture: the face of God and the face of Moses each reflects the other. Read this verse a few times and then close your eyes to meditate on it. What kinds of images come to your mind as you meditate on this text? What would happen if you took the place of Moses? Write your responses here.

What is living between your face and Jesus' face? Where are you living in the mirror? One way to know is to consider what I call circular thoughts that live in our heads. Where do you revisit sin or failure? Do you spend much time reliving past successes? Ask the Lord to bring these past trials and triumphs to mind. Sometimes our circular thoughts begin with words like, "I should have..., "I ought to have...," "If only I had..." You fill in the rest.

_____

_____

_____

_____

_____

_____

_____

_____

_____

_____

_____

_____

_____

What do you say about yourself as you look in the mirror? Do you compare yourself? Are you critical of yourself?

_____

_____

_____

_____

_____

_____

_____

_____

_____

_____

They looked to Him and were radiant, and their faces will never be ashamed (Psalm 34:5).

ENDNOTES

1. Brennan Manning, *Abba's Child* (Colorado Springs, CO: Nave Press, 1994, 2002), 97.

2. Henri J.M. Nouwen, *Life of the Beloved* (New York: Crossroad, 1992), 27.

PART II

THE TABLE

From the very beginning to the final frame of biblical history—from the first to the second Adam—the table is a common symbol of God's longing desire for intimate connection. What could be a warmer or simpler emblem of God's invitation to all who will simply come to the place prepared for them? On the brilliant resurrection side of the cross, the table expresses the peace, power, and presence of the Kingdom of God. The centrality of the table is found in every culture in history and represents a communion set between Heaven and earth. Come to the table—come and dine with Christ.

Chapter Six

Being Present

A few of us who had followed the Nazarene Rabbi whose arrest had shattered the calm of Passover, stood together. We watched from a distance as darkness ebbed from the foot of a blood-soaked cross and over the city and surrounding hills—as death seemed to triumph and take possession of His body. He breathed His last and we scattered, hiding in the city, afraid we might be next. As the prophet said, *"...Strike the shepherd that the sheep may be scattered..."* (Zech. 13:7).

Then in the darkness and gloom, my thoughts turned toward a place of comfort and calm: home. If I could only get home to Emmaus—just take a warm bath and wash off the pain and disappointment from prior days.[1]

Two of us were on the road together a few days later. For me, I felt empty—in shock. Nothing seemed real any more. Hope and vision were lost, and my body could hardly support its own weight as we shuffled along the road.

We came out through the western gate of that stunned city in the early afternoon with the sun high overhead.

The road leading out of Jerusalem reminded us of His triumphant entrance only a short time before. There was no celebration this time. Now my heart was desolate as I put one foot in front of the other, walking more out of habit than hope—more out of reflex than purpose.

As we walked we tossed words back and forth across the road. You could hear only our futile, empty, disoriented words and the sound of loose pebbles and dust crunching under out feet. Soon we could hear the sound of other footsteps coming from behind us. As they grew closer, we stopped and turned around to see a man dressed as any other pilgrim for the Passover. He had been walking a bit behind us, then came alongside and joined us.

The Stranger broke the rhythm of our shuffling steps and searching conversations. We had been walking along with our heads hanging toward the ground the whole way, but now He took our attention and we looked at Him. The man looked familiar, but we didn't recognize Him.

Then, breaking His silence, the sojourner threw Himself into the dust of our walking and our words by asking, *"What are you both talking about?"* The question took me all the way back to the beginning with Jesus. It brought back the pain and shock all over again.

"Are you a stranger here? Did you miss the darkness and the execution—the murder of Jesus from Nazareth? He was a great prophet; we hoped God had sent Him as the Messiah to get rid of the pagan influences that infest our land. He did many miracles. No one has ever seen anything like the signs He did—blind people seeing, dead people raised! We thought surely He was the one sent to restore the Kingdom of God. He talked about the Kingdom all the time and now…well they crucified Him outside the city. Surely, you must have seen or heard something about this man. Now this morning two of the women who followed Jesus said that His tomb was empty and that He is alive! Then two brothers went to the tomb and told us it was true, that Jesus is alive. How can this be? We don't know what to believe."

NOW IS THE TIME

When I read the account of the two brothers on the road to Emmaus, I find it a very believable conversation. In fact, I've lived those kinds of conversations. Have you ever been in a conversation but found that the person on the other end was not *with* you? Or maybe you have not been there when someone was talking to you.

Several years ago, when Carol and I were first married and before we had children, we lived in a cozy little apartment outside Hershey, Pennsylvania. One evening, as I was checking out the horizontal capability of our living room couch, Carol called from the kitchen saying, "Sweetie, there's a cow in our backyard!"

"What?"

"There's a cow in the backyard; come and see for yourself."

"That's nice, sweetie."

"Thom! There is a cow in our backyard!"

"OK...OK." I got up and walked into the kitchen and looked out the back door only to discover a large bovine munching on grass right off the porch. Now with brilliant insight I declared, "Hey sweetie, there's a cow in our backyard!"

I wonder how many conversations and how much of our marriage I've missed because I wasn't *with* Carol...I wasn't *present.* I am finding that my intimate relationship with God is like a conversation between the two of us. I need to be present to be part of the conversation. I have come to understand that sometimes the thing missing in my conversation with God is *me!*

In the dim far past of Genesis, there was a man named Enoch. As I have studied the life of this man, I can find no great conquest—no large body of writing bearing his name (The book of Enoch is part of the Jewish Apocrypha which is a collection of non-canonical writings largely in the intertestamental period). According to our cannon of Scripture, Enoch was a man whose greatest claim to fame was that he walked *with* God. *"Enoch walked with God; and he was not, for God took him"* (Gen. 5:24). He was "taken" by God! Walking with his Creator was his soul's focus. Every moment of life flowed through that *immediacy* with God.

To say that Enoch walked with God is to say that he lived in the immediate "present-ness" of God, that every aspect of his life was lived in view of God. The writer of Hebrews also said of Enoch that *"By faith...he obtained the witness that before his being taken up he was pleasing to God"* (Heb. 11:5). The sole reason Enoch was pleasing to

God was that he walked *with* God. Enoch had more than a "witness" of God; He had obtained a *"with-ness"* of God.

What would it mean to us to obtain a "with-ness" that we were pleasing to God simply by being *with* Him? Where would religious performance be? How could fear and insecurity survive in the present-ness of God?

Beloved, we, like Enoch, are created to live in the present-ness of God—in the present moment. When we talk about the "presence of God," we seem to talk more about an atmosphere than a person. I am thinking these days more in terms of "present-ness" of God in that He is really here in and through me.

Being present with God is the cornerstone of His covenant with us. Fenelon observed,

> The heart of your life as a Christian is contained in God's words to Abraham, "Walk in My presence and you will be perfect." God's presence calms your spirit, gives you restful sleep, and quiets your mind. But you must give yourself completely to Him.[2]

This present-ness also includes our relationships to one another as humans. Many of the challenges we experience in relationships come from not being present to one another. If I am not present with you, then where am I? I may be standing here in the room with you physically, but my mind is somewhere else—in some other time frame or context. When I am not in the present with you, then I am living in the past or the future.

If we walked up to someone on the street who had even a passing familiarity with Jesus and His teaching and asked them the two most important things He taught, they would probably say, "Don't judge" and "Don't worry." So simple and clear, yet we make it complicated and we lose the present-ness of God along with the power and opportunities of the moment.

When I live in the *past*, I am dragging judgments and opinions into the room where I am physically standing with you at the moment. I cannot see you; I see only what I think about you. I have a little file that comes up in my head, and that's who you are to me. My heart considers you and our previous history, and I miss you in the present moment.

When I am not present to you, I operate on the basis of opinion rather than compassion. I may use the Scriptures as a doctrinal catalog to reinforce my opinions and judgments, but miss you and God in the midst of it all. I cast out demons in His name; I preach in His name, but He says, "You never *knew* Me." I live "head first" rather than "heart first." All this comes from living in the past rather than the present moment and being immersed in the heart of Jesus Christ.

On the other hand, when I live in the future, I tend to worry. Jesus tells us that we can't do anything about the future anyway (see Luke 12:25). He says:

> ***Do not worry*** *then, saying, "What will we eat?" or "What will we drink?" or "What will we wear for clothing?" For the Gentiles eagerly seek all these things; for your heavenly Father knows that you need all these things. But **seek first** His kingdom and His*

righteousness, and all these things will be added to you (Matthew 6:31-33).

Listen to Paul:

> *Rejoice in the Lord always; again I will say, rejoice! Let your gentle spirit be known to all men. The Lord is near. Be anxious for nothing, but in everything by prayer and supplication with thanksgiving let your requests be made known to God. And the peace of God, which surpasses all comprehension, will guard your hearts and your minds in Christ Jesus* (Philippians 4:4-7).

"Rejoice in the Lord!" When? Right now! I can be anxious for nothing because I am not thinking and worrying about tomorrow; I'm living in the present moment with God...now! Therefore, in everything, even things that don't seem praiseworthy at the moment, I can be thankful to God with the result that peace overwhelms me beyond my understanding and overrules my "head first" approach to life. I am present and He is present. Now!

When I worry, I am divided, living in two places at once.[3] God is a jealous God and not willing to share my attentions and affections. The Jesus approach is much more tenable: *Don't judge* (live in the past), *don't worry* (live in the future), *seek first* (live in the present—be present).

This formula takes us all the way back to the beginning conversation with Jesus and His first question: *"What do you seek?"* Do we seek something from God without God Himself?

How is it that the two brothers on the road to Emmaus did not fully recognize Jesus? Simple; they were not in the present with Him on that road; their heads and hearts were somewhere else. They lived in the past and the future, but missed the present moment with Jesus right there on the road. In their conversation they said, Jesus "*was* a prophet." *Was* is about the past. They also said, "we *hoped*," which is about the future. They saw Jesus as a failure, a victim, when the Victor of victors stood right there with them!

These two followers, like us, were disappointed. Disappointment happens when we see or hope for one thing and something else happens. When our vision or plans are unfulfilled, we become *disappointed* from our expectations and lose hope. What we do not see is that the Lord is in the middle of it all the time, even when we don't see Him. *Darkness is not dark to Him* (see Ps. 139:12). We are preoccupied with our own plans and purposes. Such was the case with these two precious and bewildered brothers on the road to comfort.

There is evidence in the original text that Jesus had walked with them for a little while before the conversation erupted between the three of them.[4] He was there and they did not know Him because they were somewhere else. Perhaps they were remembering His teaching or some great miracle. Maybe all they could think of was the gore of His death a few days earlier, and nothing in them indicated that He was anything but dead.

What about all the teaching? They had heard all the words and even the several times when Jesus had told them what needed to happen, that he was going to taste death. But they lived according to their understanding of the Torah and His teachings rather than their intimate experience with the Teacher. They heard the words, but their hearts were far away in some other time zone. They did not live *now* in the present.

Beloved, *now*—the present—is where the life is. *Now* is the time of intimacy—no, immediacy. We see intimacy as a feeling and an end in itself. But immediacy brings a total connection and vulnerability—a oneness with the heart and purpose of God where past and future are crucified with Christ, where *"It is no longer I who live but Christ who lives in* [and through] *me..."* (Gal. 2:20).

Now is the time of obedience and the release of grace for the moment and the true power of the Gospel. The power of the Gospel is not for me to get what I want, but for me to become like Christ who was, above all, obedient to the Father. This oneness with the Father was modeled as a way of life by Jesus. Oneness became the greatest prayer request of Jesus, that we would be one as He and the Father are one (see John 17:20-21). Immediacy means that there is no hesitation in obedience, but a simultaneous movement like me and my shadow on a sunny day.

Little children have no trouble living in the now. They are not much concerned with yesterday or tomorrow unless it's Christmas. Jesus said:

> *Truly I say to you, unless you are converted and become like children, you will not enter the kingdom of heaven. Whoever then humbles himself as this child, he is the greatest in the kingdom of heaven* (Matthew 18:3-4).

The call and urgency is to live as children with all the sense of excitement in the moment, like on Christmas morning. Jesus is what's under the tree. Children know how to be present in the moment. Children have not yet forfeited their imaginations to the dregs of the past and the worry about the future. I think of my grandchildren. When they are here, they are really here. When they are really here, so am I. Children are into the present moment, and in the present moment is the fullest availability of the Kingdom of God. The Kingdom is now! He is Lord of the present.

With this present-ness comes humility. Humility is the awe of the present moment with God. Who can boast in the awesome presence of God—*"who may abide the day of his coming, and who may stand when He appears?..."* (Mal. 3:2). He appears each moment in the present.

Above all, *now* is the time of rest. What else is Jesus talking about when He invites us saying,

> *Abide in Me, and I in you. As the branch cannot bear fruit of itself unless it abides in the vine, so neither can you unless you abide in Me. I am the vine, you are the branches; he who abides in Me and I in him, he bears much fruit, for apart from Me you can do nothing* (John 15:4-5).

To abide is to be present—to be restfully available to Christ. This present and abiding life is a life beyond and out from under circumstances, a life filled with the lordship of Christ. When I live present to God, every moment is filled with eternity. In each moment of the present, eternity unfolds all around us. It is the life that is fruitful, not just in things accomplished, but in reproducing the very DNA of the Christ-life in us.

Jesus was into *now*. In fact He described Himself in the present tense. Listen to His list of names.

- *I am* the bread of life (see John 6:35).

- *I am* the light of the world (see John 8:12).

- *I am* the door (see John 10:7).

- *I am* the good shepherd (see John 10:11-14).

- *I am* the resurrection and the life (see John 11:25).

- *I am* the way, the truth, and the life (see John 14:6).

- *I am* the true vine (see John 15:1).

I can't see Jesus getting distracted and looking at His watch saying, "Well, got to go now." When He was with His followers, He was really with them. Jesus was at once present with the Father and the present-ness of the Father. The prophet said:

> *"Behold, the virgin shall be with child and shall bear a son, and they shall call His name Immanuel," which translated means, "God with us"* (Matthew 1:23).

When people saw Jesus, they saw the Father. Jesus said, *"Have I been so long with you, and yet you have not come to know Me, Philip? He who has seen Me has seen the Father..."* (John 14:9). Jesus was present to the Father and to those around Him and, therefore, able to see and connect with the tremendous need around Him as no one had ever done. This was the pattern repeated over and over again.

> *...He **saw** a large crowd, and felt compassion for them and healed their sick* (Matthew 14:14).

Seeing—living in the present moment—is the key that unlocks compassion, which is the very glory of God. When I *see,* I am moved with compassion, releasing the grace and mercy of God in the moment.

Beloved, we too are on a journey toward home. We have been seeking rest in a superficial way just as those two brothers who just wanted a hot bath. Christ is on this path with us, though we have not always recognized Him fully. We have been trying to find a hot bath and superficial rest, and He wants to bring us to the place of total rest and connection in His present-ness. Stop and listen now. Do you hear footsteps?

JOIN *the* JOURNEY

Where have you been disappointed in your life—where were you counting on one thing happening and something else came along? Recall the two followers on the road to Emmaus with Jesus. He was there all along, yet they were not able to see Him.

> *And while they were conversing and discussing together, Jesus Himself caught up with them and was already accompanying them. But their eyes were held, so that they did not recognize Him. And He said to*

them, "What is this discussion that you are exchanging [throwing back and forth] *between yourselves as you walk along? And they stood still, looking sad and downcast"* (Luke 24:15-17).

Read these few verses to yourself aloud in a low tone. What kinds of images or words stand out to you? Put yourself in the picture now. Can you see yourself on the road with Jesus? He has been there all along with you, even when you were disappointed. What is it that has your attention so that you don't see Jesus? What preoccupies your heart? Write anything that comes to mind here.

_____

_____

_____

What is the discussion going on in your heart? These are the words and thoughts that continually come to mind and often reflect areas of disappointment. Disappointment happens when we have appointed one thing to happen and it does not come about—where my vision and plan are not what God had in mind. List a few disappointments that come to mind.

_____

_____

_____

Now be bold as you stand on the road to Emmaus with Jesus and ask Him about those disappointments. Write anything you sense Him speaking to you concerning those specific areas of disappointment and submit them back to Him.

_____

_____

_____

_____

ENDNOTES

1. Emmaus was a place of hot springs, a place of physical comfort and rest. EMMAUS, (e-ma'-us), (em'-a-us) (Emmaous, derivation uncertain, but probably from chammath, "a hot spring"): Josephus (BJ, IV, i, 3) says: "Now Emmaus, if it be interpreted, may be rendered 'a warm bath' for therein is a spring of warm water useful for healing." (from *International Standard Bible Encyclopedia*, Electronic Database Copyright © 1996, 2003 by Biblesoft, Inc. All rights reserved.)

2. François Fenelon, *The Seeking Heart* (Jacksonville FL: SeedSowers, 1992), 121.

3. The Greek word translated "worry" is *merimna,* which means to be taken in two directions at the same time.

4. Kenneth S. Wuest translates this, "Jesus Himself having drawn near, was walking with them as they journeyed along." Kenneth Wuest, *The New Testament: An Expanded Translation* (Grand Rapids, MI: Wm. B. Eerdmans Publishing Company, 1994).

CHAPTER SEVEN

AT THE TABLE

We lifted our eyes off the ground beneath our feet and turned toward the Stranger who stood still between us. As He looked at us, first one then the other, He said, "This is foolish. You are not thinking right—you haven't put it together. You have not believed *all* the Scriptures have said. Let's talk about this together. Didn't the Scriptures clearly say that the Messiah was going to have to suffer death in order to conquer it?"

"Foolish?" His words cut through the despair, causing us to open wider to some desperate possibility that there was more than our sunken hope. "Slow of heart to believe *all*..." What could we have missed?

Then the Stranger began to put things together for us in the Scriptures. The words flowed like a fountain from the very beginning in the Torah through all the Prophets. He recounted the promises to Abraham and covenants with His people Israel and the words through Isaiah about the Servant. As He spoke, our hearts were warmed and becoming settled. What He said began to put the pieces together for us from Adam to Abraham—from Moses to Malachi. The pain of loss that had been so heavy was fading into the background and hope was rising. His words were like a fragrant balm—a refreshing spring healing our deep thirst after a long drought. All the while, as He talked, He seemed more and more familiar to us.

It was getting later in the day and we were growing closer to home. His words warmed us like a fire and we didn't want the conversation to end. Now His comforting words blended with the familiar sites and fragrances of home. Home and rest were footsteps away. As we turned toward home, the Stranger took steps as if to continue on in another direction. "Where are you going?" I asked. "You can't leave us now. You must come home with us. I insist! There is food and a place to rest. Please, don't leave us alone. We have to continue this conversation. Come with us. It's getting late and you should eat. It's been a long walk. Please come to our home...to our table."

THE UNIVERSAL TABLE

In recent years, I have had the great opportunity to travel for ministry outside the continental United States. Wherever I have traveled for whatever reason, I end up at a table with folks. I have gone to the Yucatan in Mexico several times and especially like the way many of the folks do church together. There is a time of worship with music and dancing and then a teaching time. After a further time of ministry, the chairs are cleared away and tables are set up.

Then the grandmas take over and food begins to flow. We spend a few hours together at the table eating, which seems to be the most important part.

A short while ago I had the opportunity to lead a healing experience with some beautiful Korean folks. The activity of the first few hours sealed them in my heart. The first thing after picking me up at the airport was to go straight away to a Korean restaurant where we sat for hours as they brought little dishes of food I could not recognize or pronounce. But the food was great! Each time we were together for a couple days, food was not far away. The table was always being set.

I have favorite foods now in several languages from Sydney to the Yucatan and favorite faces that go with the food. There are some language barriers in each place (even Australia) and variations of culture, but the barriers come down when we are at the table with those who will come. The table is a place where the communication is simple and direct—where there can be laughter and connection with people who don't even speak the same languages.

Our lives seem to be built around the table. When someone is born, we celebrate at the table. When we graduate college, we come to a table. We meet new people, and we come to the table. We go out on a first date, and we go to dinner. If someone dies, we go to the table. Whoever and wherever we are, life flows from and around the table.

The image and concept of the table has permeated our language and culture. In fact, when we think about it, much of world culture has evolved around table manners. The table is part of our language too. When we are being honest with each other, we say we are "putting it all on the table." If we are not being honest, we are "dealing under the table." The table is a place of connection and vulnerability, even with our enemies. Even when we cannot agree on a particular issue, we "come to the table" and share life. Listen to this ancient Bedouin saying: "I knew who they were when I saw them at the table."

During the course of our prayer counseling ministry, we have found that the table where we grew up very often tells us a lot about our families and how we see ourselves. The table can be a place of meeting and family intimacy or one of fear to be avoided at all costs. In our ministry we have found that our family tables form some of our earliest memories and impressions about intimacy and vulnerability.

We have even discovered that where we sat at the family dinner table sometimes held great significance and portrayed the level of relationships within the family. For example, we have often found that the oldest son sat to the right of the father if he was present at the table while the oldest daughter sat to the right of the mother. We could also see various roles developing at the table. Some children were the peacekeepers while others were entertainers. Some came to believe they were responsible to be the providers while others had no role we could discern. Sometimes we would see a mother sitting between a father and one of the children for whom relationship was a struggle. One way or another, the family table could be a source of rich and joyful connection or a sign of dysfunction in relationships.

What was your table like? Did your family talk together? Maybe it was not such a pleasant place—a place where children should

not be heard. Was your table filled with laughter and grace or perhaps negative expectations? Where did you sit at the table? Do you
remember where anyone else sat? What is your table like now? Are
your children dining on sour grapes handed them from your table?
Think about your family table then and how you see intimacy now.

Once I ministered to a couple struggling with intimacy of all
kinds. One of them valued and longed for intimacy, and the other
seemed to avoid it. I asked them a simple question, "What was it
like growing up around your table?" One of them described the
family table as a place where an alcoholic father made life at the
table unpredictable and chaotic. The table was a place to be avoided
at all costs. Intimacy, therefore, was not such a good idea; in fact, it
was something to be avoided.

It was a different story for the spouse who grew up in an Irish
Catholic family where parents and children laughed and talked for
hours at the table. To this family the table and intimacy were a good
thing. In realty, both of these precious people longed for intimacy,
and each projected their idea of intimacy onto the other. To one the
table and intimacy represented sweet fellowship while to the other
it was sour grapes.

The table in Scripture and in our lives represents a place of
coming to rest. It is a place of security and invitation, grace and
acceptance, provision, transparency, transformation, redemption,
community, and true identity. It is the place of *coming home* with
God and one another where we can take a deep breath and be present with one another. The table represents intimacy, which involves
openness and trust, encouraging vulnerability and the exchange of
life from the simplest to the most complex. The table is where we see

and are seen by one another. When we add it all up, the themes of the table in Scripture are *peace, power,* and *presence.*

I can imagine the conversation with Jesus and the two on the road toward Emmaus when He opened the Scriptures to them. This was the Artist explaining every brushstroke of His masterpiece. He must have walked through the familiar words of Scripture, putting a picture together of the Father's intention of intimacy and fellowship. He would have talked about the circle dance of relationship among Father, Son, and Spirit and the reality that people were created to join the dance![1]

Now, after Jesus walked through the Scriptures, He brought them to the supreme object lesson for His mission—the very emblem of communion and oneness: the *table.* Throughout history and especially in the Bible, the table has been an earthly picture of Heaven's reality. The table in Scripture represents the *peace, power,* and *presence* of God. These include the facets of rest, fellowship, provision, belonging, sharing, sonship, grace, and related aspects of God's love.

The Scriptures and history of God and His people Israel are written around the table so to speak. Listen to the first words of the Bible:

> *In the beginning God created the heavens and the earth. The earth was formless and void, and darkness was over the surface of the deep, and the Spirit of God was moving over the surface of the waters. Then God said, "Let there be light"; and there was light* (Genesis 1:1-3).

At the very beginning, even in the first lines of Scripture, God is at a table within Himself. Elohiym, the *Father,* had it in His heart to create. Then the *Holy Spirit* disrupted and vibrated over the deep darkness of early chaos. With the declaration of *"Let there be Light,"* Christ the *Son* illuminated the darkness. Father, Spirit, and Son are joined together in agreement as at a table. The table first, and foremost, is about *presence,* whether God to God, God to person, or person to person.

PRESENCE

Throughout the Scriptures the table represents a place of *presence* or present-ness where those at the table are present to one another. The Scriptures tell us that God walked with Adam in close fellowship. Genesis 3:8 says that God came to fellowship with Adam *"in the cool of the day"*—dinnertime! Perhaps the pre-incarnate Christ came and sat at a table with Adam and Eve to talk about the day's events. I see a table in Eden.

In ancient times the table could be as simple as a leather mat thrown onto the floor of a tent.[2] The table is the emblem of hospitality and coming together. To the ancients, hospitality was a duty through which the host took responsibility for the comfort of his guests. Those guests may have even been former enemies, but if they sought hospitality in the tents of the host, he would have to provide for them for several days and literally take the responsibility for their lives in his hands. At the center of these traditions was the table.

LIVING *the* GOD-BREATHED LIFE

I imagine that it was at this kind of a primitive table, a leather mat thrown onto the ground, at which Abram received the three visitors who dropped by for lunch at Mamre.

> *Now the Lord appeared to him by the oaks of Mamre, while he was sitting at the tent door in the heat of the day. When he lifted up his eyes and looked, behold, three men were standing opposite him; and when he saw them, he ran from the tent door to meet them and bowed himself to the earth, and said, "My Lord, if now I have found favor in Your sight, please do not pass Your servant by. Please let a little water be brought and wash your feet, and rest yourselves under the tree; and I will bring a piece of bread, that you may refresh yourselves; after that you may go on, since you have visited your servant." And they said, "So do, as you have said." So Abraham hurried into the tent to Sarah, and said, "Quickly, prepare three measures of fine flour, knead it and make bread cakes." Abraham also ran to the herd, and took a tender and choice calf and gave it to the servant, and he hurried to prepare it. He took curds and milk and the calf which he had prepared, and placed it before them; and he was standing by them under the tree as they ate* (Genesis 18:1-8).

Some, including me, see the three who were revealed in the circle dance of creation as the same three who visited Abram. In any event, the Lord Yahweh was not alone for lunch. Abram's first instinct was to wash their feet from the dust of a journey and then to set the table with bread of fine flour and a *"tender and choice calf."* Abram provided a table for the one who came to tell him of the seed who would be born and through whom the covenant promises of God would flow.

The table is seen throughout the life of Abraham and his seed. When Abraham won a great victory in battle, he came to a table with the king of Salem.

> *Then after his return from the defeat of Chedor-laomer and the kings who were with him, the king of Sodom went out to meet him at the valley of Shaveh (that is, the King's Valley). And Melchizedek king of Salem brought out **bread and wine**; now he was a priest of God Most High. He blessed him and said, "Blessed be Abram of God Most High, possessor of heaven and earth; and blessed be God Most High, who has delivered your enemies into your hand." He gave him a tenth of all* (Genesis 14:17-20).

This Melchizedek is a representative of Christ in the Old Testament, according to Hebrews 5:7-10. The table is synonymous with covenant in ancient times and immersed deeply in the Hebrew Bible and culture.

Consider the feast seasons God commanded His people to observe: Passover, Pentecost, and Tabernacles. (See Leviticus 23 for a complete description of the feasts of Israel.) Each one begins and ends with a Sabbath rest, and each one involves aspects of the table. Passover represents *peace* with God through the blood of the

Lamb. Pentecost represents the *power* of God through the giving of the Law and the outpouring of the Spirit following the ascension of Christ in Acts 2. The theme of Tabernacles is dwelling in the *presence* of God in booths, as prescribed by the Law. The booth or sukkah is the dwelling place for the family in the presence of Yahweh. The predominant article of furniture in the sukkah is the table.

Each feast season was celebrated with a fellowship meal in the presence—at the table with Yahweh. At Passover, Moses was commanded to observe the Pesach meal, consuming a lamb without spot or blemish, which foreshadowed Christ. Whenever the people of God came together in His presence, there was a table.

Consider the tabernacle in the wilderness constructed by Moses. This tabernacle was built in three parts around three tables. In the Outer Court, which was the place of sacrifice, there was a bronze altar for the slaughtering of sacrificial animals. This altar and all altars, for that matter, are the *table* of God (see Exod. 27:1-8). In the Holy Place was the *table* of showbread. Ultimately, in the Holy of Holies there was only one article of furniture—the ark itself, and on top of that ark was the mercy seat. The Mercy Seat is actually a picture of a *table* with cherubim facing and inclined toward each other. It was at the Mercy Seat—the table of God's *presence*—that Yahweh would meet and speak with Israel (see Exod. 25: 17-22). The images of the table and the temple continue throughout the Old Testament, including Ezekiel's visions of the temple of God where His priests would serve at His table (see Ezek. 44:16).

The image of the table is seen throughout the Torah. At one point in Exodus 24:9-11, Moses and the elders of Israel ate and drank in the presence of Yahweh, as if at a table. God's desire is clear:

He wants to be present with His people Israel. God said that Moses talked to Him as a man does with his friend, face-to-face as if both were seated at the *table* (see Exod. 33:11).

At the beginning of the reign of David, the great king of Israel wanted to consolidate his spiritual and political power by bringing the ark of God's presence to Zion where He lived. Failing to take a cue from the Philistines, who had moved the ark of God on a cart, David constructed a brand new cart to carry the presence of God into the city. This plan had tragic results. A man named Uzzah reached out to steady the ark, which seemed to be unstable on the man-made cart, and God struck him dead on the spot. (Uzzah represents the strength of man.) David was angry and afraid at the same time and decided to move the ark to the house of a simple man we know as Obed-Edom. They brought the ark to his house and parked it there (see 2 Sam. 6:1-11). I can imagine them bringing in the ark of God's presence and placing it in that humble dwelling. It was the house of a Gittite, a gentile! God is saying, *"Everyone, come to the table!*[3]

The Scriptures say that God prospered Obed-Edom in everything. Obed learned about living at the table with God (see 2 Sam. 6:10-12, 1 Chron. 13:13-14). What a resume Obed had—one who dwelt at the table of God. He began life as an outsider—a stranger to the covenants of God. But then, at the very table of God, Obed became a worshiper (see 1 Chron. 15:16-21). Obed became the doorkeeper in the house of God, with all the riches of the king available to Him (see 1 Chron. 16:5,38; 26:4-8). He ministered in the presence of God at the Ark. All this happened because the presence of God—the table of God—came to his household.

The table is seen in many places in the life of King David. There is the touching account of David, in a demonstration of the mercy of God, bringing the crippled son of his intimate friend Jonathan to his table in Second Samuel 9:1-13. Mephibosheth's father Jonathan had been killed in battle. Mephibosheth was dropped by his nurse and made lame in both legs as she was running in terror. He was helpless and powerless, living on the lookout in a borrowed tent on the side of the hill in Lo-Dabar. When David sent for Mephibosheth he said, "Don't be afraid. I will restore all that is yours and by the way, you are going to eat at my own table." *"...So Mephibosheth ate at David's table as one of the king's sons"* (2 Sam. 9:11). Inviting Mephibosheth to his table was a sign of David's security and also a simple gesture of mercy to the son of his close friend. All this young man would ever need would flow from the table of the great King David.

When we talk about the table of the Lord, we are referring to His *peace, power,* and *presence,* even in the midst of difficulty. David, aware of all of these aspects of the Shepherd of Israel, penned, *"You prepare a table before me in the presence of my enemies..."* (Ps. 23:5). Some of the downfall of the nation of Israel was that they doubted the Lord's ability to *"prepare a table"* for them in the wilderness. *"Then they spoke against God; They said, 'Can God prepare a table in the wilderness?'"* (Ps. 78:19)

As Jesus walked and talked with the two on the road to Emmaus, they were seeking some kind of physical comfort—a superficial rest from the disappointment and disaster they had known in prior days. As Jesus took them through all of history and Scripture, He showed them the *table*. Beloved, He draws us now into the journey and the conversation at His table.

In order to get to this place of very present-ness with Christ at the table, a few things were necessary. First, there was a point of transition where the two saw Jesus headed in another direction and insisted that He come with them. There was a point of urgent invitation. "Please come..." We must also invite Him with the same urgency.

Along with the table talk between Jesus and the two desperate followers came a transition from head to heart—from the merely rational to the revelation of the eternal intention for intimacy. The revelation is nothing short of the revelation of the Kingdom. At the table the Kingdom is unveiled. The table and the Kingdom of God are both within us.

JOIN *the* JOURNEY

Let's take a little closer look at your table. What was your table like growing up? Did your family talk together? Was your table filled with laughter and grace or perhaps negative expectations? Where did *you* sit at the table? Do you remember where anyone else sat? Draw a little diagram here if you like. Answer the questions and describe what it was like to be at your family table.

_____

_____

_____

_____

_____

What is your table like now? How do you think your family table affected your value of closeness and intimacy today? Think about your family table and how you see intimacy now.

_____

_____

_____

_____

_____

ENDNOTES

1. The first term used to describe the relationship among Father, Son, and Spirit was *perichoresis,* literally a circle dance.

2. The Hebrew word for table is *shulchan,* which covers a wide variety of tables from a leather mat on the floor to the table of showbread in the tabernacle. It describes more the function than the specific design of the table.

3. Obed-Edom's name suggests the Hebrew word *ebed,* which is translated "servant." This seems to be the required attitude to sit at God's table.

CHAPTER EIGHT

TWO JOURNEYS

As we traveled and talked together, the Stranger seemed more and more familiar to us. It was getting later in the day and we were growing closer to our home. His conversation resonated with us, and we didn't want it to end. As we turned toward our home, He took steps to continue on in another direction. We both insisted that He come home with us. "Please, don't leave us alone. We have to continue this conversation. It's getting late and you should eat. It's been a long walk. Please come to our home…to our table. Please…please come."

It is becoming popular today to acknowledge that we are all on a journey. We hear it everywhere from the "psycho-Babylonians" to car commercials. We tend to think of the journey as going somewhere to get something. We, like the two on the road to Emmaus, are on a journey with Christ. It is not a journey to *get*, but to *become*. It is not a journey of acquisition, but one of surrender and increasing decrease.

Along the way of this journey, we also come to a moment of transition—a turning point. It is the moment when we invite and insist that Christ come to dwell with us as those two brothers did on the road to Emmaus. In fact, the transition and our urgent invitation come moment by moment.

Transitions can be filled with pain. When my wife Carol was in labor with our children, there was a time of transition when the baby was going from a baby who lived in a womb to an individual with a brand new kind of life in the visible world. Those seasons of transition in the birthing process are a time of intensity when life hangs in the balance, when the baby is suspended between being and not being and will come forth by the sheer will and grit of the mother. Such are the transitions in the spirit and heart arena.

Beloved, we are at that moment of transition and urgent invitation even now as you read these words—suspended as the infant coming to birth. A further level of intensity and Christ-awareness awaits us. Will we ask Him to join us at our table? He will come.

There comes such a transition on our spiritual journey where we transition from babes, seeking the familiar comforts of the womb and predictable religious experience, to individuals who express the heart and presence of Christ.

These events on the road to Emmaus represent the transition toward a deeper journey. It is the journey toward true and continuous conversion when my life goes from being about me and getting something to hosting the presence of Christ—when obedience goes from being external to internal—when life goes from outer conformation to inner transformation. That moment of transition begins when we say to Jesus, *"Come..."*

TWO JOURNEYS

As the two followers walked along with the Stranger, a strong connection began to form between them because of His words. You can almost see the three of them coming to the unbearable point of separation when they invited, no insisted that Jesus would come home with them. Up until that moment, the two were seeking relief from the trauma of shattered hope—a physical comfort and rest from the outside and circumstances. Emmaus represented home and rest in a physical, external sense—a respite from disappointment and mourning—a return to what was familiar and comforting. The truth is that those external familiarities never brought true rest.

Because of a deeper hunger, they invited the Stranger to the table—to entertain something beyond their natural and normal understanding. It was a risk.

We are addicted to comfort, especially in the westernized world. Somewhere along the way the Bride of Christ insisted on a life without pain and struggle, and no longer represented the biblical description of the church. She became her own weaker sister. The church became a life foreign to the apostle Paul and the others who got this whole thing going in the first place. It is foreign to Jesus who said that as long as we are in the world there will be struggle, but that we are not subject to it because He has overcome the world (see John 16:33). It was not that Jesus ignored the world or pain; He did not allow them to distract His focus from the Father and the Kingdom to be established. He was out of this world even before the cross (see John 17:11).

I used to imagine that Jesus would steal off to a quiet place to refuel in the presence of the Father, as though He was just empty and needed to be filled up. Now I see a different image in the spirit. Now I see Jesus, who was filled with the Father, going off to a place away from the distractions and allowing the Father's life and voice *within Him* to be heard. I have gone to the quiet place to be filled up again from what has been depleted from me. But, in truth, I am coming to see that I am filled with Christ and *He* is filled with all the anointing I need. No longer am I separate and separated from Him, but He is living in me and through me! I have all the Christ I need; I merely turn to Him.

There is a comparison in Jesus' first encounter with the disciples in the Gospel of John and the encounter on the Road to Emmaus. The two journeys are seen by comparing the first two followers of Jesus (see John 1:35-39) and these two who would end up at home in Emmaus (see Luke 24:13-25). Here is a quick comparison. Both involve two followers on a road to a table with Christ. One is a journey of outward *conformation* and the other a journey of an on-going inner *transformation*.

JOURNEY OF CONFORMATION
JOURNEY OF TRANSFORMATION

We pursue Jesus.	Jesus pursues us.
Jesus says, "Come."	We say, "Come."
We abide in Christ.	Christ abides in us.
Obedience is a method.	Obedience is a response.
We go where Jesus lives.	Jesus goes where we live.

When the first two disciples began to follow Jesus in John 1:35-39, they knew there was something beyond their present experience and launched after Jesus in pursuit. That desire to pursue was put there by the God in whose image they were created. We do not seek God because it's a good idea. We seek Him because we are created to do so—to know Him.

As I said in an earlier chapter, what the two were pursuing was rest, a place of abiding connection and availability in God. This extends to the followers on the road to Emmaus before the transition point where they invited Jesus to come home for dinner. Everything they were concerned and talking about was on the outside: their thoughts of a kingdom military takeover and a militant messiah who would kill Romans and heal Jews. Through the time they had followed Jesus on His earthly ministry, they had not yet connected at a heart level. Like abandoned children, they were only concerned with their loss and seeking the comfort of this world.[1]

On the outward journey we are concerned with finding relief from the stuff of daily living—we come to God for what He can do. We are preoccupied with the signs and circumstances because of our deep need for affirmation. On the outward journey we are following Jesus to His table—coming to receive something from Him. We come restless and needy and depend upon Him to meet those needs. We come with a certain experience and understanding or opinions. Though we seek a deep rest, we settle for superficial and circumstantial relief like the two on the road with Jesus. They would have been content with ending Roman occupation without having really experienced an inner transformation.

On the inward journey we come to know that Christ is seeking us. Our desire for the immediacy of abiding connection with God is part of our original nature.

Our desire to follow Christ started with Him, not us. A.W. Tozer wrote:

> We pursue God because, and only because, He has put an urge within us that spurs us to the pursuit. *"No man can come to me,"* said our Lord, *"except the Father which has sent me draw him."* (John 6:44), and it is by this prevenient drawing that God takes from us every vestige of credit for the act of coming. The impulse to pursue God originates with God, but the outworking of that impulse is our following hard after Him. All the time we are pursuing Him we are in his hand.[2]

JESUS SAYS, "COME;" WE SAY TO JESUS, "COME"

In the outer journey we are responding to an invitation by Jesus to *"Come."* Remember in the first conversation in John 1 that the followers asked *"Where do you live—where do you abide?"* Though they were referring at that moment to a physical dwelling, Jesus did not *live* there. Jesus abides in the Father and the Father in Him. When Jesus invites them and us saying, *"Come and see,"* He is not inviting us to a place as much as an exchange of life—our life with all its fits and starts to His abundant life. He is inviting us to Oneness with Him and with the Father.

> *The glory which You have given Me I have given to*
> *them, that they may be one, just as We are one;* **I in**
> **them and You in Me**, *that they may be perfected in*
> *unity, so that the world may know that You sent Me,*
> *and loved them, even as You have loved Me* (John
> 17:22-23).

Have we come to a point where we are dissatisfied with life and our relationship with Christ and are willing to invite the "Stranger" to our table? Are we willing to not let Him go and to invite Him to come and find His home in us? Maybe this was what was happening as Jacob wrestled with the angel, whom I believe to be the presence of Christ, all night until He blessed him. (See Genesis 32:26.)

Our transformation and the journey inward begin when we say, "Come...."

OBEDIENCE IS A METHOD; OBEDIENCE IS A RESPONSE

It was never God's plan that His people operate like robots, carrying out His laws and decrees. It has always, even in the days of ancient Israel, been about living in personal awe of God first and from that, arising obedience. The habitation of Christ in us is what leads to true obedience of heart and His Kingdom being expressed through us.

> *Now, Israel, what does the Lord your God require*
> *from you, but to* **fear the Lord your God**, *to walk*
> *in all His ways and love Him, and to serve the Lord*
> *your God with all your heart and with all your soul,*

and to keep the Lord's commandments and His stat-
utes which I am commanding you today for your
good? (Deuteronomy 10:12-13)

To fear Yahweh is not to tremble at the threat of reprisal or retribution from our sin, but to be in awe to the point of entire focus.
It is the feeling we get when we see some wonder beyond our scope
and experience. Imagine that you have never seen the ocean and
then walk onto the beach to see the vast and boundless water, to
hear its roar. I felt this kind of awe when we visited a region in Australia called Katoomba. When we arrived there, we got out of the
car and made our way to an overlook. At once I caught sight of the
sprawling canyon in the Blue Mountains. It took my breath away. I
was in awe. I became richer, yet small at the same time.

Notice in the text that, when we are living in awe of God,
walking in His ways, serving with our whole hearts, and keeping
His commandments and statutes follow naturally. Obedience is
not merely a following of instructions, like our kids who pick up
their dirty clothes off the bedroom floor because they want to go
to the mall. There is an inner obedience of the crucified heart that
is becoming the heart of Christ—a heart vibrating with the same
heart and desire of the Father.

We obey because of the one who lives in us. As Paul said:

I have been crucified with Christ; and it is no longer
I who live, but Christ lives in me; and the life which I
now live in the flesh I live by faith in the Son of God,
who loved me and gave Himself up for me (Galatians
2:20).

WE GO WHERE JESUS LIVES; JESUS GOES WHERE WE LIVE

This has been the plan of Heaven all along—a life in which God lives *through* us. It has been a mystery now revealed in and through the Church. The first journey is one of living in Christ. The second and inward journey is one where He lives in us!

> *If anyone loves Me, he will keep My word; and My Father will love him, and We will come to him and make Our abode with him* (John 14:23).

> *I am the vine, you are the branches; he who abides in Me and I in him, he bears much fruit, for apart from Me you can do nothing* (John 15:5).

Beloved, the main question is whether we will invite Jesus and give Him the place at the head of our table, which is to say our lives. We are at the place of transition where the momentary is:

> *"...crucified with Christ; and it is no longer I who live, but Christ lives in me; and the life which I now live in the flesh I live by faith in the Son of God, who loved me and gave Himself up for me"* (Galatians 2:20).

In 1994 the *New York Times* carried the story of a man who learned about carrying the heart of an indwelling and loving presence. A middle-aged man who had experienced the failure of his heart was placed on a heart transplant list as a last hope. He and his family had been waiting on this list for some period of time when tragedy struck the family. The man's 22-year-old daughter was killed in a car accident. Prior to her death in the accident, the young woman had signed up as an organ donor so that in the event of her death someone would be able to find life through her organs. Neither she nor anyone else ever expected the way her wish would be fulfilled. As it turned out, the young woman was a match with her father as a donor. Upon her death, her heart was harvested and was transplanted into the chest of her father.

The experience and all the incredibly complex emotions must have been overwhelming—probably still are for all those concerned. We know for sure that this father understands what it is like to carry the heart of someone he loved deeply. How careful would this father be to take care of the heart of a precious daughter? With each heartbeat, he would be reminded of the love of his daughter. Her heart was abiding in his chest. This is the journey of transformation when Christ abides in us.

As we say, "Come..." to Jesus, He will come. He will come to my house and to my table. My table—my life—will become His. Amen! *Come Lord Jesus!*

ENDNOTES

1. Emmaus was a place of hot springs, a place of physical comfort and rest. EMMAUS, (e-ma'-us), (em'-a-us) (Emmaous, derivation uncertain, but probably from chammath, "a hot spring" (from *International Standard Bible Encyclopedia,* Electronic Database Copyright © 1996, 2003 by Biblesoft, Inc. All rights reserved.)

2.   A.W. Tozer, *The Pursuit of God* (Camp Hill, Pennsylvania: Christian Publications, 1982, 1993), 11-12.

CHAPTER NINE

THE TABLE AND THE KINGDOM

When we got home, we washed and sat down at the table together. There was bread on the table before us, and I motioned to take it, expecting to say the traditional blessing. Before I could get hold of it, the Stranger took the loaf of bread in His own hands and lifted it up before us speaking the blessing, *"Blessed is the Lord our God King and Creator of all Who brought forth this bread from the earth."*

When He took the bread and blessed it, He began to break off pieces for us. As He handed me a piece of bread, I saw His face and hands more clearly. The wounds were still visible. Suddenly—immediately—illumination brilliant as the sun dawned on the parched landscape of incomplete knowledge. Something like a great tidal wave of understanding broke upon me, satisfying an indescribable, eternal thirst. *All* the words that the prophets had spoken came crashing into their present reality as their Messiah sat before us. It was no stranger; it was Jesus!

I remembered His words a few days earlier at the Pesach Seder, "I will eat this bread again with you when the Kingdom has been established." I opened my mouth to shout His name, and at that moment He disappeared from my sight.

We could not stay where we were; we had to go and tell the others, even at the risk of a long journey back to Jerusalem in the approaching darkness of night. This news was too big—too important. The other followers had to know that it was all true that Jesus was alive! When we arrived at the meeting place, we burst into the door and shouted, "It's true!! He has risen! He is alive! We walked with Him and then He sat with us at the table and when He broke bread we saw that it was Him...at the table as He was with us all so many times before—at the table."

Just then Jesus was standing there with us. I don't know how; He was just there. Some of the followers thought He was a ghost. But He calmed us down and said, "I'm no ghost—I'm real. Go ahead and touch Me. Here, I'll prove I am real." He walked toward the simple olive-wood table and reclined saying, "Bring Me something to eat...ghosts don't eat, do they?" He ate right in front of us. As He sat at the table, it all came together.

Now Jesus said, "All that I have done, all that was written through the Torah, the Prophets, and other Writings has been to bring us together at this table." Then Jesus breathed on us and said, "Receive the Holy Spirit—the Spirit that will remind you of Me and this table. It was all about being at this table with you from beginning to end. All the teachings...all the miracles...all the pain was about this. This is what the Kingdom looks like. I was at the table with My Father before time began. *And just as My Father has granted Me a Kingdom, I now grant you the right to eat and drink at My table in My Kingdom.* Now stay together at this table until I send power to you— power to bring others to My table" (author's interpretive translation, see Luke 22:29-30).

From the very beginning and throughout His ministry on earth, Jesus brought us close to Himself. His first public sermon indicates as much, "Repent, change your ways of thinking, and trust now in the heart of God. The Kingdom is at hand; it's right here and right now. The Kingdom is inside you" (author's paraphrase, see Mark 1:15). For Jesus, the Kingdom of God was more like a warm banquet with the King, and everyone was invited.

In the final days of His earthly ministry, Jesus addressed the nearness of God and the Kingdom.

> *Asked by the Pharisees when the Kingdom of God would come, He replied to them by saying: "The kingdom of God does not come with signs to be observed or with visible display, nor will people say, 'Look! Here [it is]!' or, 'See, [it is] there!' For behold, the kingdom of God is within you [in your hearts] and among you [surrounding you]"* (Luke 17:20-21 AMP).

Jesus was concerned with nearness—with being close. The table was a constant in the days of His earthly ministry. It was the arena of nearness. Jesus transformed the experience of the Kingdom of God from an external concept to an inner reality, making it part of us. He made Himself part of us. Jesus was a man who hung out at the table at every opportunity. Jesus was so often at the table that His critics and religious detractors called Him a glutton (see Luke 7:34). The table was the great object lesson and platform to reveal the heart of Heaven. From first to last, Jesus has been feeding the Kingdom to His disciples then and now at the table.

FROM THE FIRST...

Many of the "firsts" in Jesus ministry happened around a table of some kind. When Jesus took the first two followers home with Him in John 1:35-39, He brought them to His *table*. That simple image of hospitality set the attitude for His ministry of access, vulnerability, and transformation which is true intimacy. The table made a strong statement: "This is where I am...This is where I long for you to be."

The first miraculous work Jesus performed was at a wedding feast—*a table* where He turned water into wine (see John 2:1-11). In doing so, Jesus was taking on the role of the Host providing wine for the guests—*at the table*.

The first name Jesus called Himself also suggests the table. Jesus declared to a mystified group of followers, *"I am the bread of life; he who comes to Me will not hunger, and he who believes in Me will never thirst"* (John 6:35). If we come to Him, if we trust Him, we are removed from mere physical appetites because we have all we need in Him. Jesus is the center—He is the bread of true life.

When Jesus called followers, He was calling them to come to the table. One day as Jesus was walking along, there was a misplaced Levite named Matthew whose very name suggests that he was born to be a disciple.[1] The name Levi suggests that he was from the tribe that served in the temple in the presence of God.

> *After that He went out and noticed a tax collector named Levi sitting in the tax booth, and He said to him, "Follow Me." And he left everything behind, and got up and began to follow Him. And Levi gave a big reception for Him in his house; and there was a great crowd of tax collectors and other people who were reclining at the table with them. The Pharisees and their scribes began grumbling at His disciples, saying, "Why do you eat and drink with the tax collectors and sinners?" And Jesus answered and said to them, "It is not those who are well who need a physician, but those who are sick. I have not come to call the righteous but sinners to repentance"* (Luke 5:27-32).

I can almost hear a conversation something like, "What's a nice Jewish boy like you doing in a place like this?" Notice that the first thing that happened following Matthew's conversion was a reception at his house. Matthew, Jesus, and all of Matthew's associates came to a table. There was a wide assortment of the disenfranchised at the table—people who would not have felt welcome in the synagogue service. Jesus' message of the Kingdom is that everyone is welcomed at the table—into the Kingdom. Imagine the shocking surprise it must have been to bring Jesus, a radical rabbi, to the dinner table. Matthew's friends showed up because they were probably curious. Of course the religious "stick in the muds" did what they do best. They grumbled and complained and conspired about the fact that Jesus would sit at the table with sinners. In fact, it was the only table He had gotten an invitation to. Matthew's table instantly became Jesus' table—an expression of the Kingdom of God.

The first time Jesus was invited to talk by the religious types was at a table (see Luke 7:36-50). A Pharisee named Simon invited Jesus to recline at his table. Simon's table was designed more as a trap to ensnare Jesus rather than a place of intimacy. Once at the table, a woman known only in the text as "a sinner" came up behind Jesus and began to worship at His feet, washing them with her own tears and anointing them with precious oil. Simon responded with doubt and revulsion saying, "If this man was really a prophet, he would know what kind of person is touching Him! The truth was, *He did!* He knew exactly what kind of person touched Him, and she was welcomed. Jesus went on to tell the parable of the two debtors who were forgiven. The one having the greatest debt gave the greatest thanks and praise. Then Jesus forgave the woman at the table! Forgiveness is removing something from the table so there is no longer any obstacle to intimacy, whether God to person or person to person. This woman took the role of a servant and washed and anointed the feet of the guest. A new order was established, and Simon's table became the table of Christ, and the Kingdom was seen by all.

Jesus was anointed at a table again, this time for His burial with costly perfume (see John 12:1-8, Mark 14:3-9). The others were indignant that this woman *"did what she could"* by anointing Him at the table. Her ministry of anointing was a touching gesture in humility. Jesus said of her, *"And truly I say to you, wherever the gospel is preached in the whole world, that also which this woman has done shall be spoken of in memory of her"* (Mark 14:9). In the whole world, whenever folks gather at the table, they should remember the fragrance of this service.

In the John 12 version, there is another significant table reference. In verses 9-11, many came to the table to see Lazarus. Jesus had become so identified with the table by this time they knew just where to find Him. This account of the anointing by Mary begins earlier when Jesus raised Lazarus from the dead and earlier still with the relationship between Jesus and this family from Bethany, who had a long history of table relationship.

> *As Jesus and the disciples continued on their way to Jerusalem, they came to a certain village where a woman named Martha welcomed them into her home. Her sister, Mary, sat at the Lord's feet, listening to what he taught. But Martha was distracted by the big dinner she was preparing. She came to Jesus and said, "Lord, doesn't it seem unfair to you that my sister just sits here while I do all the work? Tell her to come and help me." But the Lord said to her, "My dear Martha, you are worried and upset over all these details! There is only one thing worth being con-*

*cerned about. Mary has discovered it and it will not
be taken away from her"* (Luke 10:38-42 NLT).

This visit is another table encounter. It is set during the Feast
of Tabernacles where the people of God were to live in a sukkah,
a small hut woven from various branches. Tabernacles represent
God's desire that His people would dwell in His presence. Martha
and Mary had a brother named Lazarus (whom Jesus raised from
the dead, as told in John 11).

During Jesus' visit, it is likely that Lazarus was doing what every
other pious Jew was doing; he was in Jerusalem observing the Feast.
Before he left for the Feast, he and his family would have constructed the traditional sukkah and would have dwelt there.

During the Feast of Tabernacles, the sukkah was the primary
dwelling where the family rested and ate together. It was a place to
focus on the presence of God.[2] The touching scene of Jesus' visit
becomes clearer when we see Martha scurrying back and forth from
the house to the sukkah while her sister Mary was seated at the feet
of Jesus while He was *in* the sukkah. There is a single piece of furniture in the sukkah: a *table*. As Jesus reclined at the table, Mary was
positioned behind Him in a posture of utter humility, waiting on
His every movement and word—ready to receive and to respond in
a moment. The table is the place of restful and purposeful availability in *peace*—a place of trusting in the *power* of God for provision, a
place to experience the intimate and immediate *presence* of Christ.
The table and all that goes with it are the *"good part, which shall not
be taken away"* (Luke 10:42).

Jesus' equating the table with the Kingdom must have become obvious to others around Him. The table expresses the reality of the Kingdom in a way that everyone would have understood and identified with. In the Gospel of Luke, the table became a lesson on humility and generosity in the parable of the guests (see Luke 14:7-8). Here's my paraphrase of Jesus' teaching: "Take the least important place at the table. It's not about you." Jesus was saying that the table is about generosity and that you should not invite only those whom you love and who can repay you.

The Kingdom is not about position or title or performance; it's about being at the table of the King! He has not invited us to His table so that we can repay Him. How could we possibly repay Him? Therefore, invite the crippled and lame to your table, those who cannot get there on their own. They cannot repay you either. You are at the King's table by invitation and grace, not because you've earned a spot. It was obvious to at least some that Jesus was equating the table and the Kingdom. *"When one of those who were reclining at the table with Him heard this, he said to Him, 'Blessed is everyone who will eat bread in the kingdom of God'"* (Luke 14:15).

The table teaching continued as Jesus told the parable of the invitation (see Luke 14:16-24; Matt. 22:2-15). The table was set and invitations were sent out, but nobody showed up. They all had more important things to do and gave one excuse after another. Jesus' teaching was clear. There is still room for anyone who would come to the table. He has sent His Servant, the Holy Spirit, out to get us and bring us to the table. The Master has sent out to the side streets and back alleys to bring us in. The Kingdom and the table are not about appearances. *"Blessed is everyone who will eat bread in the kingdom of God!"*

...TO THE LASTS

The table was the arena of His final teaching, where Jesus taught them the table manners of the Kingdom of God (see Matt. 26:20-29; Mark 14:17-25; Luke 22:1-18; John 13-17). *"When the hour had come, He reclined at the table, and the apostles with Him"* (Luke 22:14). "The hour"—the moment of the greatest transition in the history of the world finds Jesus at a table with those He loved so deeply. The table and the elements of communion were the final teaching about the Kingdom. Jesus said, *"I have earnestly desired to eat this Passover with you before I suffer; for I say to you, I shall never again eat it until it is fulfilled in the kingdom of God"* (Luke 22:15-16).

Indeed, the next time Jesus would eat this meal was in Emmaus, after He was resurrected in victory over sin and death. The purpose of His sacrifice and all He had done was to bring them and us back to the table of fellowship.

The values and lessons of the Kingdom were poured out in the final meal this side of the cross. Jesus chose the table with the simple staples of bread and wine as the way to place a marker. He said:

> *"This is My body which is given for you; do this in remembrance of Me." And in the same way He took the cup after they had eaten, saying, "This cup which*

is poured out for you is the new covenant in My blood" (Luke 22:19-20).

The table was shorthand for the Kingdom. Each time they would come to the table, there would be an association with Jesus and His nearness. To *"remember"* Jesus was to put it all back together again. They would recall His words and His attitudes. "The Kingdom is here! The Kingdom is at hand! The Kingdom is like sitting with Me at this table!"

Here are a few of the pure and simple directions and lessons that came from His time at this final table:

Remember Him (see Luke 22:19).

It's a new day with a new covenant (see Luke 22:20).

The greatest ones serve (see Luke 22:27).

It's His table (see Luke 22:30).

Wash each other's feet (see John 13:14).

Love one another (see John 13:34,15:12,17).

Believe in Him (see John 14:1).

He has made a place for us (see John 14:2).

He has sent the Spirit to the table to remind us (see John 14:26).

He gives us peace (see John 14:27).

If we abide in Him, He will abide in us (see John 15:5).

We are His friends (see John 15:14).

He has overcome the world (see John 16:33).

In a final and unequivocal association of the Kingdom and the table, Jesus said, *"Just as My Father has granted Me a kingdom, I grant you that you may eat and drink at My table in My kingdom..."* (Luke 22:29-30). (A painting of Jesus' last meal with his followers hangs over our dining room table with this passage inscribed at the bottom.) To seal the deal, Jesus made a final gesture of humility, which describes our attitude in coming to the Kingdom. He washed the feet of those who sat at the table with Him so often. He emptied Himself, doing what the lowest servant would do, not insisting on His rights, but choosing to love and serve in this intimate way. He is the example of true humility.

> *Have this attitude in yourselves which was also in Christ Jesus, who, although He existed in the form of God, did not regard equality with God a thing to be grasped, but emptied Himself, taking the form of a bond-servant, and being made in the likeness of men. Being found in appearance as a man, He humbled Himself by becoming obedient to the point of death, even death on a cross* (Philippians 2:5-8).

Jesus showed Himself at a table many times after He rose from the dead. The first time He was recognized after His resurrection was at the table in Emmaus. As Jesus sat at the table with them, He took the bread in His own hands and said the blessing, *"Blessed are You, the Lord our God, King of the universe..."* When Jesus lifted up the bread at the table, He was saying that the fall and its curse were now reversed, that God was again the Provider. People would no longer live by the sweat of their brows physically or spiritually. The

King and His table had been established! Now the *peace, power,* and *presence* of God had been reestablished and the table of Eden restored.

Jesus continued to minister at the table as He breathed the Holy Spirit out on His followers in John 20:22. He was reviving them with the same breath that had been knocked out of them at the fall in Eden. Jesus proved to His shocked and delighted followers that He was real by eating food at the table. You can almost hear them saying, "Look, it has to be Jesus. He is still eating at the table!"

The ministry of the table did not end when Jesus ascended to Heaven. The Holy Spirit came as Jesus said He would, and it was at the table. The followers of Jesus were gathered together, as at a table, in the upper room on Pentecost when the Holy Spirit came upon them as tongues of fire. The power of the Holy Spirit came to empower them to bring the whole world to the table (see Acts 2:1-4). And they did.

Beloved, a great and ultimate feast awaits us. We have been invited to the final event that will never end, the culminating fellowship of eternity at His table—in His Kingdom!

> *Then he said to me, "Write, 'Blessed are those who are invited to the marriage supper of the Lamb...'"* (Revelation 19:9).

JOIN *the* JOURNEY

Have you ever received an invitation to a fancy, formal dinner? I recall one such time when I was invited to come to a dinner at a friend's house. When I arrived, I was shown a large table and taken by the hand to a specific chair. On the table, in front of that chair was a little card with my name on it. I was invited and expected. There was a place assigned for me. So it is with the table in the Kingdom of God. You are invited and expected. There is a place setting there just for you.

Take a moment and reread the Scripture on the previous page from Revelation 19:9. This text is talking about you! Meditate on the reality of this table and invitation. Can you close your eyes and envision yourself being taken into the banquet hall to this table? What does it look like to you? Describe it here.

Now, someone has greeted you and taken you by the hand and led you to this banqueting table. What would it feel like to be taken in such a way to this table? Imagine that there is a card on the table with your name written on it in gold. What would you feel as you see your place at the King's table? Describe that here.

_____

_____

_____

_____

Spend some time at the table with Christ today. Just be there and meditate on Him and the invitation. Take communion today with your family at the table. Make it Christ's table. When you've taken communion together, write down any thoughts or impressions here.

_____

_____

_____

_____

_____

_____

ENDNOTES

1. Matthew Levi, probably from the tribe of the Levites.

2. Alfred Edersheim paints a picture of the likely scene of the visit of Jesus to the sukkah of Lazarus, Martha, and Mary in Bethany in *The Life and Times of Jesus the Messiah* (McClean, VA: Macdonald Publishing, 1883), Book IV, Chapter V.

CHAPTER TEN

TURNING THE TABLE

The Stranger took the loaf of bread in His own hands and began to say the blessing. "Blessed is the Lord our God King and Creator of all who brought forth this bread from the earth."

Imagine that you and a few friends are meeting in a Starbucks for morning coffee. The conversation and the coffee are warm and inviting—so much so that another person in the nearby table falls into the conversation with you, and you all begin to talk as though you had known one another for years. When it comes time to leave, you mention to your other friends that you are hosting a little gathering at your home that evening. It seems appropriate and right to you that you also invite your newfound friend, though no one knows him very well. Maybe you've seen him around this Starbucks before, but never connected. Now you invite him to the gathering, and he accepts your invitation.

That evening the hour of the gathering arrives, and you find your new friend at the door. You welcome him into your home and to your table and everyone including your Starbucks buddies says hello. In a few minutes you move to the table and you are about to welcome your friends with a blessing when suddenly the new friend stands up and says a blessing over the table and friends as if it were his table. What would be going through your mind and heart if this happened to you at your table?

To us, it may have seemed a rather forward or maybe even a rude thing to do, but this is what happened when Jesus, the Guest, took the bread into His own hands and spoke the blessing at the table in Emmaus. But something far more significant than a simple table grace took place as Jesus blessed the bread. With His blessing their table became His table. Jesus was taking His rightful place as Head. There was transference of sovereignty.

No doubt Jesus spoke a blessing similar to what is still spoken today among the Jewish people at the table. Jesus said, *"Blessed are You, O Lord, King of the Universe who brings forth bread from the earth."* This blessing acknowledges not just the bread, but the one who provided it. When Jesus said these words, there was a turning of tables and kingdoms. Jesus was in effect saying, "It is all now as it was in the very beginning before sin and doubt entered the world. Everything is back in place again."[1]

Bread is representative of life in Hebrew thought. Bread was the essential staple of the ancient world. God is the one who creates the grain and rain to produce bread. Both His bread and His Word are life to us.

For as the rain and the snow come down from heaven,
and do not return there without watering the earth

> *and making it bear and sprout, and furnishing seed*
> *to the sower and bread to the eater; so will My word*
> *be which goes forth from My mouth; it will not return*
> *to Me empty, without accomplishing what I desire,*
> *and without succeeding in the matter for which I sent*
> *it* (Isaiah 55:10-11; see also 2 Corinthians 9:10).

God is the source of bread and, therefore, life. He gave bread/life to the Israelites in the form of manna in the wilderness, as described in the Torah (see Exodus 16:31). Jesus, the Son of God, created a feast of bread for thousands out of somebody's lunch in the Gospels (see Matt. 9:15-19). The statement is clear: "I am the source of bread and, therefore, the source of life. I am the Bread of Life."

When Jesus took the bread into His hands and blessed it, there was transference of ownership. He was taking back into His hands what got out of hand in Eden. Jesus was invited as the Guest, but took the role as Head of the table. He was turning the table.

My table is my personal kingdom—the domain of my soul—the place where I live. The bread is my life, with all its trials and circumstances that live on at the table. Sometimes I try to manage my Christian life by adjusting the table manners to be more "Christian." But what is needed is that my table becomes the table of Christ.

There is a progression that leads to turning my table into Christ's table. The Lord first invites me to *intimacy,* face-to-face at His table. When I am there, He reveals Himself as He always does, and I fall in love with who He is rather than what He can do for me. I see who He is and how He sees me. My table is becoming His table. The bread of my life is in His hands. That is the definition of *humility.*

Now, being secure and safe at His table, I am free from the need to perform and prove my worth because it is a settled matter. I am free to live in *obedience*. That obedience provides the *evidence* that my table has become His table—my life is now His life. It is no longer I who live, but Christ who lives in me! The progression is *intimacy*, which leads to *humility*, resulting in *obedience*, which provides the *evidence* that His table is set within me.

Coming back to the original conversation and question in our journey, we must ask, *"What do you seek?"* We seek something that was lost. What was lost to us and to Christ was the intimacy and connection we were created for—the table in Eden. When we lost this closeness and immediacy with God, we hid in the bushes out of our insecurity. We still do. The *peace* of His table has been replaced by the uneasiness of self-searching, self-worth, self-sufficiency, and all the other hyphenated trash of self-. The *power* of His table's provision gives way to what we can produce by the sweat of our brow. And now, instead of the joy of His *presence,* we are only aware of *us* and spend our lives managing the fear and the pain of living away from His table resorting to sin and self-efforts. We are *lost*.

We know that Jesus is Seeker-sensitive, that He came to *"seek and to save that which was lost"* (Luke 19:10). See how Jesus pursued a lost and orphaned son of Abraham.

> *He entered Jericho and was passing through. And there was a man called by the name of Zaccheus; he was a chief tax collector and he was rich. Zaccheus was trying **to see who Jesus was**, and was unable because of the crowd, for he was small in stature. So*

> *he ran on ahead and climbed up into a sycamore tree in order to see Him, for He was about to pass through that way. When Jesus came to the place, He looked up and said to him, "Zaccheus, hurry and come down, for today I must stay at your house." And he hurried and came down and **received Him gladly**. When they saw it, they all began to grumble, saying, "He has gone to be the guest of a man who is a sinner." Zaccheus stopped and said to the Lord, "Behold, Lord, half of my possessions **I will** give to the poor, and if **I have defrauded** anyone of anything, **I will** give back four times as much." And Jesus said to him, "Today salvation has come to this house, because he, too, is a son of Abraham. For the Son of Man has come to seek and to save that which was lost"* (Luke 19:1-10).

Can you see the throng as Jesus entered the city gates? They were abuzz because Jesus had healed the blind man at the gate of the city. Wonderful! Amazing! There were women lifting up babies for Jesus to bless, and the religious of the city were asking questions and straining to hear Jesus' reply. Now Jesus went one step further and brought home a lost son to the table of the Kingdom.

INTIMACY

There was Zaccheus, a vertically challenged man who lived on the outskirts of acceptance. He worked for the civil government and put his hands in the pockets of his neighbors. Why? Because he was lost to intimacy and the table, he had to try to be someone or prove something to himself by getting more stuff. He was addicted—he needed money and a way to feel power. This was life outside and away from the table. He was an orphan in the outer darkness, but knew he had a need. He did not know the *peace, power,* and *presence* of the table.

He was seen as tainted and unworthy, even as an enemy of his neighbors—a sinner. Zaccheus was a homeless rich man. Ironically, his Hebrew name means "pure," but he and everyone around him saw him as anything but that—everyone except Jesus.

Zaccheus was a man who felt small and powerless. What do we do when we feel this way? We try to gain altitude—to get higher. (Some just get high.) So Zaccheus climbed a tree. He could not see Jesus. The instinct and longing of Eden inside him told this lost son that there was something more that had come into his neighborhood, namely Jesus. Zaccheus was trying to *"see who Jesus was"*—not what He did, but *"who Jesus was."*

Just minutes before, the blind beggar at the gate had wanted to regain his vision, to see in a physical sense. But Zaccheus wanted to see at a deeper level. When the text says that Zaccheus wanted to *"see who Jesus was,"* the word in the original text is more like "to perceive" or "to know" beyond the simple seeing. This was a need to know Jesus. The deep emptiness in the heart of Zaccheus connected with the seeking heart of Christ.

Jesus, ever the Seeker, was aware of the one wrestling up a sycamore tree and called out the invitation, *"Come on down Zaccheus, I'm coming to live at your house, to your table today!"* I can imagine the shock and surprise in Zaccheus when he heard his name called.

"Zaccheus!!" He could not have expected it, but Jesus knew him and called him by name. He knows His sheep, especially the lost ones, and *calls them by name* (see John 10:3). This was not the call to judgment and retribution. It was an invitation to sit at the table—Zaccheus' table. Jesus did not come with a stick or a list of offenses. He just *invited* him to come down and join Him at the table for intimacy. *"Zaccheus, come down..."*

HUMILITY

It didn't take long for Zaccheus to respond to the invitation to intimacy. He did what Jesus told him to do; He hurried down the tree and *"received Him gladly."* Perhaps a better translation would be that he received Jesus joyfully.[2] To have joy is to be above the circumstances of the moment. For once someone had seen something in Zaccheus besides what he may have done. Someone knew him as a son and a person of value and worth. Jesus had to have known that this would get Him unfavorable reviews with the religious types in the crowd. They were all shocked by the invitation to this "sinner" to come down.

The essence of true humility is seeing ourselves the way God sees us. Not some false show that we put on to show folks how low we can make ourselves. *Humility is the enthronement of Christ*—giving the place of Headship at our tables and taking our place as guests at the table. Humility is the attitude that turns the table from our table to Christ's. Andrew Murray in his book on Humility wrote, "Humility, the place of entire dependence on God, is, from the very nature of things, the first duty and the highest virtue of the creature, and the root of every virtue."[3] In other words, we are giving Christ the place at the head of our table—Sovereign and Lord and, therefore, Provider.

Zaccheus brought Jesus into his home and became a guest at his own table. Humility is the condition of heart where our will— what is important and valuable to us—is subject to the one at the head of the table who is Christ. Over and over again Zaccheus used the phrase, *"I will,"* saying that whatever was Jesus' will had become his will—whatever was important to Jesus was now important to him. He no longer needed to take advantage of people by sticking their money in his pocket. He was somebody—he was *present* with Christ at the table. Humility came from intimacy, not the other way around.

I have to wonder if the indignity of the religious folk around Zaccheus was because they had never thought of bringing Zaccheus to their tables. It was so simple, yet it eluded them. They were a little defensive and preoccupied with the sin of this tax gatherer. They could not *see* Zaccheus past their own insecurities.

OBEDIENCE

The invitation to *intimacy* at the table brought about the attitude of *humility,* which leads to a response of *obedience.* The Hebrew thought behind obedience is the idea that we have heard God speaking and are now going to respond.[4] As I said in an earlier chapter, when I'm in the flesh, obedience is more like a means to an end. But when I'm at the table, obedience is a response to the Sovereign at the head of the table. I am not my own; I have been bought with a price and, therefore, glory only in Christ with all He has entrusted to me. Notice that Jesus did not have to spell out a list of penalties and consequences to Zaccheus. Because the table of Zaccheus was now the table of Christ, everything on that table— all his resources—belonged to Christ. Zaccheus simply obeyed the heart of Christ and did what Jesus would have done. Words in this case were not needed.

Zaccheus was not trying to hold anything back or plead to a lesser offense with Jesus. Justice flowed from the intimacy at the table. Zaccheus did much more than was required by the law to restore. The law would have required him to pay twice, but he determined to pay four times anything he had gotten through unrighteous dealings. This was not mere restitution; it was restoration of a son of Abraham to his place at the table.

EVIDENCE

When Jesus was about to ascend to His throne in Heaven, He gave specific instructions to his followers who had been at the table with him so many times before. He said something like, "You all wait here—right here at this table, and I will send you power from Heaven. This power will so change you that you will no longer be your old frightened selves; your lives will be the evidence that I am who I say I am to people even in the remotest parts of the world" (see Acts 1:6-8). I supply the word *evidence* over *witnesses*, which is used in most English translations. *Evidence* is given to bring about truth and justice in a court of law. No where are we called to witness, but to be witnesses of Christ—the evidence of His transforming *peace, power,* and *presence.*

Imagine the impact this changed life must have had on the folks in the neighborhood who knew this little crook as an enemy. Now he was generous. Now Zaccheus was living from the table of Christ. Jesus said, "Today salvation, healing, restoration, identity, joy has come to your table. Your table is My table! On My table there is no lack—no reason to defraud anyone. Everyone is welcome, and there is enough for everyone who comes." I wonder how this affected the generosity of Zaccheus and his family. I can imagine that Jesus was not the only guest who came to the table at Zaccheus' house. I see no reference to Jesus telling Zaccheus to get another job. He continued on in his occupation, but now with integrity. He, like Obed-Edom, lived from the table with Christ. This was the evidence of transformation and the transference of sovereignty of the table in the house of Zaccheus.

I don't play the shame game, asking you if there is enough evidence to convict you of being a follower of Christ. Salvation, healing, respect, identity, and authority come with our place at the table. So ought we to live. The followers of Jesus in the Book of Acts were a community of people who lived at His table. This was an amazing Kingdom bunch of guests at the King's table who claimed no thing as their own and had all things in common. This was true community based on living at the table of Christ! No one had lack of anything because they had it all in Christ at His table. That alone is enough to turn the world upside down.

Beloved ones, we are invited to intimacy at the table. As those two followers on the road to Emmaus, we bring Jesus to our table.

He longs to take the bread, our lives, into His hands. When my table, my kingdom, become His table, then He will *take* me, *bless* me, sometimes *break* me with the purpose of removing what stands in the way of our intimate relationship, but will then *give* me as evidence of the nearness of His Kingdom through my life.

Jesus invites me to *intimacy,* and as I see Jesus, *humility* arises; once my will is out of the way, I live in *obedience*; with obedience my life becomes the *evidence* of His life and heart. He has turned the table from my table to His.

JOIN *the* JOURNEY

I have occasionally felt like Zaccheus, small in stature and unable to see who Jesus is.

> *Zaccheus* [Your name here] *was trying **to see who Jesus was,** and was unable because of the crowd, for he was **small in stature**. So he ran on ahead and climbed up into a sycamore tree in order to see Him, for He was about to pass through that way* (Luke 19:3-4).

Put yourself in the place of Zaccheus. What would you imagine he felt as Jesus was passing by and he could not see Him? Are there times when you feel small and cannot see? What does that feel like to you? Maybe you can think of a recent time when you felt something like Zaccheus felt; write it here. Describe what happened and how you felt about it. Then ask yourself why you felt that way. This will uncover what you believe about this event.

Now invite Jesus to your house and table. Can you sense anything He might say to you as He comes to your house and table?

_____

_____

_____

_____

_____

_____

_____

_____

_____

_____

_____

_____

_____

_____

_____

_____

_____

_____

ENDNOTES

1. The ancient rabbis believed at one time that before people sinned, God provided everything, that even bread grew on trees and people did not have to labor for it.

2. The Greek word *chairo*, which means with cheer or joy.

3. Andrew Murray, Humility, The Beauty of Holiness, (Los Angeles, CA: IndoEuropean Publishing, 2009), 2.

4. The Hebrew word for obedience is *shema*, which is also translated as "listen" or "hear." Obedience is the proof that we have heard God.

CHAPTER ELEVEN

NO LONGER ORPHANS

But when the fullness of the time came, God sent forth His Son, born of a woman, born under the Law, so that He might redeem those who were under the Law, that we might receive the adoption as sons. Because you are sons, God has sent forth the Spirit of His Son into our hearts, crying, "Abba! Father!" Therefore you are no longer a slave, but a son; and if a son, then an heir through God (Galatians 4:4-7).

A DAUGHTER'S STORY

Eileen is a young woman in her early 20s who is bright and beautiful and excited about life with her young son, Joseph. Life ahead of her is filled with light and love, though it was not always so.

Eileen was born to a mom who struggled with alcohol in Baltimore City. As her mother's addiction grew out of control, she was no longer able to deal with the challenges of a small child. So when Eileen was one and one-half years old, her mother had to release her to the "system." She was at the mercy of a system that, despite their best efforts, could never provide a home and real family. Meanwhile, in another part of the state, there was a young couple named Ron and Lisa who already had children but were feeling a stirring to bring another child into their home to love as foster parents. Within a short time they were approved to receive a child and a cute little 1½-year-old girl named Eileen arrived. It was always their goal to see that child adopted by another loving family. They had no idea that an opportunity to meet adoptive parents would come up so soon.

One Sunday morning they took little Eileen to church where, lo and behold, another family came forward asking to adopt her. Rich and Laura were thrilled, and the adoption soon took place. Things went well for a few years, but when Eileen turned six years old, her adopted family split up, leaving Eileen with a single father and two brothers. Young Eileen was lost in the middle of this family-quake. A few difficult years went by, and when Eileen was 13 years old, her adoptive parents were remarried. But by this time, having been abandoned several times, Eileen began to struggle and became an untenable challenge to her parents, who were no longer able to cope with her. Once again Eileen was abandoned to the "system."

Through her teen years, Eileen shut down to the idea of family or hope of another adoption, though there were a few opportunities. There was a faint murmuring somewhere in the recesses of her young heart of that first young couple, Ron and Lisa, who had loved her into their family. Longing for her own family, an 18-year-old Eileen became engaged to a young man, and the couple soon found out they were pregnant. The young man refused the child as his own and walked away, ending the relationship. Once again, Eileen was sent away—abandoned.

Shortly after this, she began searching for home again. Eileen found Ron and Lisa's daughter on MySpace. This connection led her back to Ron and Lisa, who felt like home to Eileen. She had been allowed to sleep on her birth mother's couch until her son was born, but had few prospects for a future life for her son or herself. She wanted and needed a home and family. Not coincidentally, Lisa began to experience that same stirring she had felt when Eileen was a small child to come alongside and provide a safe place for Eileen and her newborn son. Eileen wanted to "come home." Lisa drove to the city and picked up Eileen and her infant son. While they were driving out of the city, Lisa looked in the rearview mirror of her car and watched the skyline grow smaller behind her. She grabbed Eileen's hand and said, "This is a new day—a new beginning for all of us."

Ron and Lisa brought these two lives to their table. Eileen had been abandoned or sent away many times during her early years. There was a cycle of abandonment in her life that could only be broken one way: someone had to invite her to take her own place at their table. Eileen continues to struggle occasionally because of the years she spent in the darkness away from the table. But she has an invitation to the King's table where all that she needs is provided.

Like Eileen, we all have a longing in us for home and a place at the table. We were born homesick. This longing is like a GPS leading back to the Father's heart. From the nerdy kid in the lunchroom to the secret emptiness of the executive lost in his or her career, we long to be chosen—to be invited to the table of belonging. Without this connection we are orphaned—alone in the outer darkness.

When we hear the word *orphan,* we may think of a child living along the sidelines and outskirts of family. In its ancient roots the word we translate "orphan" refers to someone living in the outer darkness, as if away from the table. There was a man, a musician, in ancient Greek mythology named Orpheus whose name comes from the same root. In his story, Orpheus lost his beloved wife to death. He was grieved, and a torrent of mournful songs flowed from him. As the story goes, Orpheus descended into the darkness of the underworld called Hades to find his wife, though in the end he could not bring her back. In the end Orpheus was alone in the outer darkness.

Though we may know at some level that we are children of God, sometimes we live as spiritual orphans. We live away from the table. The farther we are from the table, the dimmer the light. We spend much of our lives trying to deal with the darkness, in pursuit of a place at the table. We sometimes feel disconnected and alone in the dark. We live with orphaned minds in orphaned churches filled with orphaned hearts.

There are many notable orphans in the Bible, such as Esther or Ruth, who became an orphan by choice. Mephibosheth, the son of David's best friend Jonathan lived far away from the presence of the king and his table. In the end, his greatest healing was David's invitation for Mephibosheth to come and eat at the king's table as a son. David adopted him, saying, "Do not fear. I will restore. Come to my table."

The table is a place of peace, provision, grace, community, belonging, and acceptance, but mostly a disarming nearness of community which leads to rest. In that rest is our identity as children of

God. Think about your table growing up. Did you or others around your table tend to sit in the same place? Was there an order? Did you feel as though you had a role or secure place at the table?

Jesus went around gathering up the outcast ragamuffins of the world and making room for them at the table. We are like those ragamuffins still living with orphaned hearts. We are still trying to earn a place that is freely ours for the accepting. Why is it then that we do not find rest and our place at the table? The apostle Paul described the difference between the way sons and orphans come to the table.

> *Remember that you were at that time **separate** from Christ, **excluded** from the commonwealth of Israel, and **strangers** to the covenants of promise, having **no hope** and **without God** in the world. But now in Christ Jesus you who formerly were **far off** have been **brought near** by the blood of Christ* (Ephesians 2:12-13).

Separate, excluded, strangers, no hope, far off...these words describe the life of the orphaned heart. The comparisons and contrast between children of God and those with an orphaned heart could fill a book or two. Orphans feel alone and don't have a strong sense of identity. Children or sons are a vital part of the table. The future of the family flows through them. The table they sit at will someday be theirs, and their children will sit there too.

Those who live with orphaned hearts live without the intimate awareness of God, while children sit at the table face-to-face with Him. Those who live away from the table tend to hide their hearts and focus on themselves out of sheer desperation. Sons and daughters are free and secure in love at the table. They can live with open hearts, not allowing pain or offense to fester and become bitterness, which might cause them to push away. They are intentionally "brought near" to the table simply because they are loved.

Those with orphaned hearts spend their lives trying to earn a place at the table through performance and, therefore, seldom enjoy the intimacy and sharing of the table. Children are at the table by invitation and have a place with their name on it.

Orphans often come to *get* something at the table, like beggars snatching a morsel of food and then scurrying back into the darkness to eat it. Children come simply to connect.

The orphaned heart is clothed in rags of self-effort and uncertainty while the children of God sit at the table clothed in Christ.

Finally, those with orphaned hearts live in desperation, seeing life as an exercise in survival. They are like street children looking in the shop windows or homes, not knowing where their next meal will come from. They are at the mercy of a merciless system. Life becomes a battle with no hope in sight—no warmth or touch. They *live by bread alone,* waiting for the next crumb of affection and connection. But the children at the table live out of the intimate sense of connection with the Father at the table. Free from the life of search and seizure, they are able to focus on the one who set the table, so they live God-breathed lives filled with hope.

Here is a quick chart for contrast:

Orphans	Sons
Feel excluded and alone	Included as heirs
Don't know the promises	Heirs to the promises
Without God	Deeply loved, accepted
Hide their hearts	Transparent hearts
Far off	Brought near
Focus on themselves	Focus on the Father's face
Perform for a place	Seated by grace
Come to get something	Come to connect
Clothed in rags	Clothed in Christ
Live in desperation	Live in inspiration

Part of our journey is wandering to find these things—to find a place at the table. We who have been far off have been brought near by the blood of Christ and the will of the Father.

Adoption means being given a place at the table as a son and heir. It is a change of identity where we rewrite the birth certificate of the adopted. When we have a place at the table, we begin to think and act like sons, no longer slaves or orphans.

In ancient times, when a child was to be adopted, there was transference of authority from one father to another. The adopted child became a new person with a new identity and a new name to go with it. Witnesses were asked to attest to the new identity of the child. All this happened simply because the adopting father was stirred to bring the child to his table just as we talked about earlier in this chapter with Eileen and her new family. In essence, Eileen was brought to their table and given a place that would never be taken away or lost.

Our adoption as children of God is not of our efforts, but originated in the very heart and nature of God, who created us for His table. *"A Father to the fatherless and a judge for the widows, is God in His holy habitation* [at His table]*"* (Ps. 68:5). Beloved, we, who are the sons and daughters of God through Christ, are being led by the Spirit of God to the table of God (see Rom. 8:14-17). He calls us chosen and beloved to His table. Jesus said, *"I will not leave you orphans; I will come to you"* (John 14:18).

The Father delights in your nearness to Him—to His table. When we take our assigned place at His table, He becomes our entire field of vision—our portion. Hear the words of one who sat at His table.

> *Whom have I in heaven but You? And besides You, I desire nothing on earth. My flesh and my heart may fail, but God is the strength of my heart and my portion forever. For, behold, those who are far from You will perish; You have destroyed all those who are unfaithful to You. But as for me,* **the nearness of God is my good***; I have made the Lord God my refuge, that I may tell of all Your works* (Psalm 73:25-28).

These are not the words of an orphan straining and striving for a place at the table, but the confident declaration of one who knew who he was—a son of the King's table and no longer an orphan.

JOIN *the* JOURNEY

Here is the comparison again. You might take a few minutes and place a checkmark next to the words that describe your approach to the table and life.

Orphans	Sons/Daughters
Feel excluded and alone	Included as heirs
Don't know the promises	Heirs to the promises
Without God	Deeply loved, accepted
Hide their hearts	Transparent hearts
Far off	Brought near
Focus on themselves	Focus on the Father's face
Perform for a place	Seated by grace
Come to get something	Come to connect
Clothed in rags	Clothed in Christ
Live in desperation	Live in inspiration

Remember Ephesians 2:13, that *now in Christ Jesus you who formerly were **far off** have been **brought near** by the blood of Christ*? If we are going to live like the children of God, we must see ourselves as such. Make these "I am" declarations over yourself as you come to the table of Christ.

"I am an heir at Christ's table."

"I am deeply loved and accepted at His table."

"I have been brought near to the table in Christ."

"I am free to focus on Christ at His table."

"I am seated by grace at His table."

"I am clothed with Christ at His table."

"I am free to be inspired at His table."

It is possible that some of these declarations don't feel true to you personally. Try picturing yourself at the table with Jesus and listen to Him speaking these truths to you personally.

"You are an heir at My table."

"I love you deeply."

"I have brought you to My table."

"You have My total attention at My table."

"You are seated at My table simply because I want you here."

"You are clothed with Me at My table."

"I long to breathe new life into you at My table."

CHAPTER TWELVE

THE GOD-BREATHED LIFE

• • • Then Jesus breathed on us and said, "Receive the Holy Spirit—the Spirit that will remind you of Me and this table. It was all about being at this table with you from beginning to end. All the teachings… all the miracles…all the pain was about this. This is what the Kingdom looks like. I was at the table with My Father before time began. *And just as My Father has granted Me a Kingdom, I now grant you the right to eat and drink at My table in My Kingdom.* Now stay together at this table until I send power to you—power to bring others to My table."

A few years back I had the opportunity to lead a retreat for a group of pastors in the Yucatan of Mexico. Several pastors and their spouses along with our team of six went to a beautiful resort for a few days. We came to the table for teaching and several meals together, experiencing this same journey that you and I are on right now in this book. By all accounts, it was a moving and successful time with these precious brothers and sisters.

When the event was over, our refreshed team got back on an aircraft to begin the journey home. I had asked the team members to journal during the time we were in Mexico concerning anything the Lord may have spoken to them on the retreat. The aircraft was only about two-thirds full, so we took time to shuffle seats around so we could share our journals and thoughts. After our sharing, I had a little listening time with Christ and a scene flashed before the eyes of my heart.

The scene was of a table where Jesus had prepared a simple meal for the two of us. We enjoyed the meal for a bit, and the scene was filled with the presence of Christ. After awhile the bread ran out, and I got up and walked away from the table. The Lord spoke to my heart and said, "Thom, sometimes you come to the table and sit with Me and all is well, but when the bread is gone you get up and turn your back and walk away from the table. Son, *man does not live by bread alone, but by everything that proceeds from the mouth of God*" (see Deut. 8:3).

That was it. It all happened in a flash. I didn't feel rebuked, but was aware of the sense of loss because I had turned my back and walked away from the table. I had missed the point. The point of all of it was Christ, not the bread.

There are two modes of living described in the Scripture Jesus quoted. One is a life of dependence on *bread,* the perishable stuff of life. The other is on the *breath*—what *proceeds* from the mouth of God. What proceeds from the mouth of God is what is inspired— *God-breathed.* We are invited to a life of inspiration—a God-breathed life.[1] I have seen that we spend most of our time looking for the *bread* on the table and seldom connect with the one who invited us to the table.

The *God-Breathed Life* is the culmination of all we have been sharing in this writing. It is the answer to the question, "*What do you seek?*" The God-Breathed Life is one of the *peace, power,* and *presence* of God. It is where we desire to live; it is a life of rest *for, in,* and *from* God; it is the longing of our hearts and what was in the heart of God before time; it is the point of the table and the by-product of Kingdom life; it is where we abide in Christ and become His abode; it is the reason we come to the table to live face-to-face with the One who so longs to see us; it is the life of the children of God who no longer live in the outer darkness of performance religion. The God-Breathed Life is our true destiny.

The word *inspired* means that God is breathing life *into* us. When God breathes, the result is life even in the midst of what looks hopeless and dead. Elohiym looked around Eden and found a patch of dry red dust. Taking it into His hands, He breathed—exhaled into it—and then formed man from the dust and the condensation of His own breath (see Gen. 2). Our life in Christ is a remnant of that first kiss of God to child at creation. We were created to live a "God-breathed" life.

God breathes life into utterly dead and hopeless things. The prophet Ezekiel looked over a pile of dead and hopeless bones.

> *The Lord took hold of me, and I was carried away by the Spirit of the Lord to a valley filled with bones. He led me around among the old, dry bones that covered*

the valley floor. They were scattered everywhere across the ground. Then He asked me, "Son of man, can these bones become living people again?" "O Sovereign Lord," I replied, "You alone know the answer to that." Then He said to me, "Speak to these bones and say, 'Dry bones, listen to the word of the Lord! This is what the Sovereign Lord says: "Look! **I am going to breathe into you and make you live again!** *I will put flesh and muscles on you and cover you with skin. I will put breath into you, and you will come to life. Then you will know that I am the Lord'"* (Ezekiel 37:1-6 NLT).

Following Jesus' resurrection from the grave, He appeared among His disciples, as we chronicled in the opening narrative of this chapter. Harmonizing the Gospels of Luke and John, we get a picture of Jesus entering the place where His followers had been secluded and speaking His shalom over them. The proof Jesus gave them that He was real and alive was coming to the table and eating something. In the course of the conversational encounter, Jesus breathed on His followers saying, *"Receive the Holy Spirit..."* (see John 20:19-23; Luke 24:36-48). The account in Luke's Gospel says that Jesus *"opened their minds to understand the Scriptures"* (Luke 24:45). He transplanted the life of His heart into His followers—a burden to bring others to the table of His Kingdom. Jesus "inspired" them.

I read recently about a study that showed that there is enough DNA in the condensation of human breath to identify the person who exhales it. When we exhale, the essence of our life is broadcast, carrying with it our DNA—our identity as individuals. Jesus *inspired* His followers and imparted the same DNA—the same life that healed the blind and raised the dead during the days of His earthly ministry—the same life within Him that gave Him the grace to say, "Not My will, Father, but yours be done" in the hopelessness of Gethsemane (see Matt. 26:39). Jesus' disciples "received"—inhaled into themselves that same breath of God, which inspired them to preach the Gospel to the outermost parts of the world. Jesus breathed into them the *peace, power,* and *presence* of God, then sent them out to bring others to the table of His Kingdom.

There is a contrast from the life of *bread* to the life of *breath*. It is the difference between what *motivates* us and what *inspires* us. Here is a brief comparison.

BREAD OR BREATH?

Motivation/The Bread	Inspiration/The Breath
Will be taken away	Never taken away
Circumstantial peace	Perfect peace
Drains me	Satisfies me
Makes me anxious	Brings me peace
Drags or pushes me	Invites me
About me	About God
Life is survival	Life is worship

Motivation flows from a formula, something like "I will _____ so that _____. However, if _____ doesn't happen then I'm done." It is like deciding to get up and walk away from the table when the bread is gone. Whatever is on the table that motivates us can and will be taken away. The "bread" will eventually run out or wear out or rot and rust. It is like all the toys we wanted when we were kids. (Or like the last time I went to the computer and electronics store.) It is not eternal. It is mere bread!

Inspiration, on the other hand, touches something in us that cannot be taken away from us any more than our DNA. I could gain or lose weight, change my clothing, or wear a sombrero, and that would change my appearance. But what has been God-Breathed into me does not change, though it may be expressed in another way. What God has breathed into us will always be a part of us—it will be our default self.

Dr. Ben Lerner, a specialist who trains Olympic athletes, observed that those who compete out of *motivation* train hard with the express purpose of winning the event they run in, but if they lose they quit. However, inspired athletes run whether they win or lose. They cannot help it; it's who they *are!*[2]

When I live for the *bread*, what I pursue can and will be taken away. When I live by the *breath*, what I pursue cannot be taken away by any calamity or circumstance because what I pursue and what pursues me is Christ.

When I live for the *bread*, I live under the circumstances; when I live by the *breath* of God, the circumstances are under Him in His perfect peace!

When I pursue the *bread,* I spend all my energy and resources getting and having and never just *being.* When I live by the *breath,* I am satisfied and His mercies are new every morning for me.

When I live for the *bread,* I live in fear of never having or being enough. Instead of seeing the possibilities of the present moment, I am hobbled by fear and lack. When I live by what proceeds by the *breath,* I live in the settled peace and confidence that all I need is before and within me in Christ.

When I live for the *bread,* I am constantly feeling dragged or pushed. When I am dragged, it is usually shame motivating me—the concern that I am missing something or have fallen short. When I feel pushed, it's usually fear that has its hand at my back, pushing me along as if at the point of a spear and prodding me to go where I do not wish to go. But when I live by the *breath,* I am invited into what the Friend is doing.

When I live for the *bread,* it's always about me and what will make me look good or feel good. It is about what I come to the table to get. When I live by the *breath,* my life is all about the One on the other side of the table who invites me to recline with Him.

When I live for the *bread,* life becomes an exercise in survival—living in insecurity and uncertainty. I snorkel my way through the sea of daily concerns, hoping to keep my head just above disaster. When I live by the *breath,* every act is one of worship—the most mundane chore is holy—done in the presence of the One who calls me chosen, holy, and beloved.

As recorded in the life and conversations of Brother Lawrence, a simple monk who served his God in the kitchen in the 1600s:

The time of business does not with me differ from the time of prayer; and in the noise and clutter of my kitchen, while several persons are at the same time calling for different things, I possess GOD in as great tranquility as if I were upon my knees at the Blessed Sacrament.[3]

When I am living by the *breath* of God, then every moment is redeemable—filled with the presence of God. But it is a choice every moment as well. We choose to trust and to listen to the voice of Christ within us. Oswald Chambers said:

If we will take the initiative to overcome, we will find that we have the inspiration of God, because He immediately gives us the power of life...If we are inspired by God, what is the next thing? It is to trust Him absolutely and to pray on the basis of His redemption.[4]

When I consider the conversation between Jesus and dear Nicodemus, I see a God-breathed moment. Jesus told Nicodemus that he and we must be born again. Later Jesus elaborated further, saying that we must be born of water and spirit, literally the *breath* to enter the Kingdom of God (see John 3:3-8). I now see Jesus saying that I must receive and be inspired by His very breath to live in His Kingdom. When Jesus said we must be born of the spirit, He was saying we must be born of His *breath*. Jesus was speaking and thinking Hebrew in this conversation; the words for spirit, breath, and wind are the same.[5]

We have confused seeing the Kingdom with what the Kingdom produces. Jesus was saying that seeing the Kingdom is a product of the new life/spirit/wind. The Kingdom could not be reduced to a thought or a movement; it was in fact a new *kind* of life "born from above."

Being born again is not merely a prayer I utter at an altar at some point, though that may be the beginning point of my yield to His reign. Being born again is a brand new life where I am solely Christ's. It reminds me of the Song of Songs where the maiden says, *"I am my Beloved's and His desire is for me"* (Song of Songs 7:10). In this declaration she was saying that her entire life was secure in the reality that she was deeply loved and desired by the King.

The *God-breathed* life is where our lives become the evidence of His indwelling presence—where we are the beloved of God. Jesus quoted the Scripture about *bread* and *breath*—that *"man shall not live by bread alone"* when He was being tempted by satan in the wilderness. Satan tried to create doubt in Jesus by saying, *"If you are the Son of God..."* (see Matt. 4:3-4). We come to believe that *if* we are affirmed as children of God, we will not experience lack or pain or loss. We doubt who the Father says we are.

Jesus' fasting was a way to quiet the hunger in His flesh in order to connect with the Father. I believe the thing that allowed Jesus victory over satan was the word of the Father that still echoed in His spirit: *"This is My beloved Son in whom I am well pleased"* (John 3:17). Do we hear and believe that we are the "beloved" of God? Our greatest doubt seems to be in who God says we are.

The *God-breathed* life is one where Christ washes worry and distraction that has accumulated on our feet from the journey—where we come to the table with nothing in our hands but an invitation—where we are inspired and carried along by His breath. It is a life of healing and redeeming past hurts and putting away the sin and judgment that preoccupies us and separates us from His face—a life of becoming the *evidence* of His reign and drawing the world to His table.

Once a religious scribe of Jesus' day tested Jesus and got a clue about the *God-breathed* life.

> *And a lawyer stood up and put Him to the test, saying, "Teacher, what shall I do to inherit **eternal life**?" And He said to him, "What is written in the Law? How does it read to you?" And he answered, "You shall love the Lord your God with all your heart, and with all your soul, and with all your strength, and with all your mind; and your neighbor as yourself." And He said to him, "You have answered correctly; do this and you will live"* (Luke 10:25-28).

The "eternal life" that the scribe was seeking is the *God-breathed* life. Jesus' simple key to the God-breathed life was a total love of the One God with all we are in every way, loving Him as if hanging on every word and quieting our hearts to hear His. But the *God-breathed* life flows as love is extended to others at the table in the community of His presence. That is why we come to the table and break the bread together—why we share the indwelling Christ with one another. Love must be shared or it is nothing more than a sentiment. Jesus said the world will see this *God-breathed* life in us as we love one another. When the world sees this evidence, they will come. *"And they will come from east and west and from north and south, and will recline at the table in the kingdom of God"* (Luke 13:29).

From beginning to end, it has always been about the table where we are no longer orphans, but sons and daughters of the King—where the most important time is now. His invitation has been engraved and is now in your hands.

Come Lord Jesus!

> *Blessed is everyone who will eat bread in the kingdom of God* (Luke 14:15).

JOIN *the* JOURNEY

Did you ever hear the words or melody of a song that you could not get out of your head? You find yourself whistling or humming it all day long. No matter what you do, no matter what other melodies come to mind, you keep coming back to that same theme. Our lives are like that. There are themes that keep coming up over and over again. There are themes that run through our activities and efforts. A theme that runs through my personal life is the table. Everything seems to come back to the table.

If your life was a song, there would be a particular melody or theme that keeps coming up. For example, you may have a longing desire to write a book or a song. You may not have training in those areas, but that desire surfaces over and over again. These desires are how God has wired you. Write down the themes that run through your life here. What has God breathed into you?

_____

_____

_____

_____

_____

_____

_____

ENDNOTES

1. Inspired, theopneustos, "God-breathed." Theos, God and pneuma, breath. In ancient times it was believed that the gods imparted divine breath to men in the form of gifts and inspiration in such things as music and art.

2. Dr. Ben Lerner, *Body by God: The Owner's Manual for Maximized Living* (Nashville, TN: Thomas Nelson, Inc., 2003), 27-29.

3. Brother Lawrence, *The Practice of the Presence of God* (Gainesville, FL: Bridge-Logos, 1999), 6.

4. Oswald Chambers, *My Utmost for His Highest* (Grand Rapids, MI: Discovery House Publishers, 1992).

5. The Hebrew word *ruach* can be translated "wind," "breath," or "spirit."

PART III

THE ENCOUNTER

Y ou are invited. Jesus now draws you into the conversation. You will continue the story and the journey to cultivate rest at His table. Now you will take up the pen and finish this book. Now comes a journey of simplification—the journey toward union with Christ where you and He will look deeply into your heart and discover His. In this continuing journey, the dust and debris of daily living will be washed away, and you will become an apostle of His Kingdom that cannot be shaken and carry the fragrance of Christ to the world.

CHAPTER THIRTEEN

THE INVITATION

Imagine with me that my wife Carol has invited you to her dinner table. (Note that although I live in the same house, it's really her table.) The menu is one of her specialties. She has prepared her now famous macadamia chicken with all the sides. She begins with a plump and fresh chicken breast which is marinated overnight in a sweet "mustardy" kind of sauce, then rolled in some crumbs, which include ground-up macadamia nuts and a bunch of other seasonings. The chicken is baked to a golden brown, crunchy on the outside and juicy on the inside. Mmmm...

The side dishes are mouth-watering as well, like green bean casserole with those little fried onion rings and the heart-clogging creamy, cheesy sauce baked until the cheese and onion rings are bubbling brown and forming a crust on the top. Maybe she made twice baked potatoes and some other obligatory green vegetable. (Hopefully not brussels sprouts.) It's going to be great. We are all in for a treat.

The setting and atmosphere are important as well. Carol has set her fancy French provincial cherry table with her fine china—dishes I am never allowed to touch under pain of death. She keeps these dishes and the silverware in a hutch that is also off limits to lugs like me. She lights a few candles on the table, which are placed in silver candlestick holders, and finishes the whole thing off with soft classical music in the background. (It probably has some "fluty" thing going on since she is a flutist.) The whole package is designed to make the guests feel special and welcome. This is going to be good.

Now the doorbell rings. It's you! Carol is excited about having you over for her multi-sensory feast. Mostly she wants to see you. She looks around and makes careful inspection of all the final details, adjusting the candle sticks and silver on the table until all is just so. Now she walks to the door as the doorbell rings a second time and opens the door. To her utter horror and surprise, you are standing there with a McDonalds' bag in your hands. No offense to "McDonald-ites," but the grease is doing to the bag what it is going to do to your major arteries in a few hours. Carol didn't tell you to bring anything, not even a bag of chips. This feast was her gift to you, and you stopped at McDonalds on the way just in case...of what I do not know.

Imagine what Carol—what any of us—would feel if we invited someone to our table and they brought a burger and fries or a pizza. You fill in the blank here. Now think about this. You have insulted my orthodox Italian wife, inferring that what she was preparing would not be good enough, and now you come to the table and sit down. (Carol has this look that I get occasionally if and when she is perturbed with me for my many inconsiderations and social stupidness. You probably got that look, but now the moment has blown over and her incredible grace has allowed you to come alive to her table.)

Dinner is served! You and the few other guests pass the entrees around the table as the sound of "Mmmm...," and the smacking of lips adds to the ambiance. We have all enjoyed a few courses, including some kind of fudge brownie at the end with some great hand ground coffee. During the meal the conversation was warm and lighthearted. Everyone is having a great time. Now when the food is all gone, you take the linen napkin by your setting and delicately wipe the corners of your mouth. You're settled as long as there is food on the table, and you sit there until the food is gone. But then you push your chair back and stand to your feet. Backing away from the table, you break eye contact and walk away saying, "Gee, thanks for the delicious dinner. It was great. Got to go now." With that you turn your back and walk out the door, leaving the other guests and the hostess breathless. You came for the food and missed the main course: the conversation!

How would you feel if you were the host? This is not an attempt to shame or make anyone feel bad. It is an account of what we miss at the table with Christ. You were invited. The food was good, but the main reason you were invited was because of you—your presence and His at the table, not what you might bring or what He could give to you.

Beloved, we have been invited to the table with Christ. We have experienced moments of warmth and satisfaction as He has prepared a place for us. But we have sometimes walked away from the main purpose of the invitation, namely the immediate and transforming presence of Christ. *He* is the point!

During this third and continuing encounter with Christ, we will come to a table and discover things that have sometimes distracted us and kept us away. We will interact with the Spirit of God who carries Christ's invitation to us. We will learn about things we have brought in our hands when all we have been asked to bring was ourselves. Among other questions, the Lord Himself will reveal...

1. *What is on your feet?* We face distractions, such as worry, that take our attention from Christ and His table. Jesus wants to wash those distractions from your feet and flush them out of your heart because they compete with Him for your attention and focus and they rob you of true peace.

2. *What is in your hands?* We sometimes try to bring a six pack and a bag of chips to the table of grace to compensate the Lord rather than simply receiving the blessings of His grace. Whatever we bring in our hands is going to have to be removed if we are to experience His table.

3. *What is in your heart?* As we sit or recline at the table, we are physically at the heart level. We will lay hold of the conversation going on in our hearts and find out what God has breathed into us.

4. *What is in your eyes?* As we sit with Christ at the table, we become aware of obstacles that rob us of the connection we are destined to have with Christ. These obstacles may be the remnants of past hurts or even sins and mistakes that have not been healed and released to the hands of Christ.

As you are on this journey, you will be keeping a log of the things the Lord reveals to your heart along the way. I have created open spaces for you to respond to the presence of Christ. Everyone's journey is a little different or maybe a lot different. There are no right answers to fill in the blank, and no one will be checking your work. This is not a test; it's a journey and an encounter with Christ at His table. You are coming to His table simply because He has invited you to come.

The setting of this encounter is Shabbat—the Sabbath that is to be a time of Rest. Rest and the Sabbath are foreign to many of us who are followers of Christ, yet it was an important part of the Law and the teachings of Christ. You will be invited to join in the blessings and the communion with Christ at His table. You are going to enter into that Rest at the table with Jesus.

The text is interactive, and you will be encountering Jesus in a live conversation. This may be a little different for some readers, as we tend to take a more cerebral and rational approach to our relationship with Christ. This encounter is more about who we are as spiritual children of God, invited and welcomed to the table with Christ, than it is about having right doctrine or practice.

You are writing the final chapter. This journey does not end with the final page of this book. It will never end, though it will traverse through stages. At best, we see Jesus and ourselves in an unclear and distorted way. *"For now we see in a mirror dimly* [enigmatically], *but then face to face ; now I know in part, but then I will know fully just as I also have been fully known"* (1 Cor. 13:12). Along the way we will come to see Christ and ourselves more clearly.

Regardless of how or why you've picked up this book, the one who created you now calls you, sending out a personal invitation to come to His table, not once for a visit, but as a lifestyle of Rest in the present-ness of Christ. This is but one step and a small beginning to the journey.

His table is set; you are invited; now come!

> *Blessed is everyone who will eat bread in the kingdom of God* (Luke 14:15).

CHAPTER FOURTEEN

MY JOURNEY TO THE TABLE

Here I am, in the middle of my daily routine with God. My daily spiritual routine consists of... (Describe your daily activity with God—how you pursue or interact with Him. This could be a daily quiet time in a regular place or an occasional thought or awareness of His presence.)

_____

_____

_____

I am a seeker and ready to leave behind life as usual for something more in the Spirit. There must be more than I have experienced from God and my spiritual life up until now. I would describe my relationship with God as... (For example, God seems near to me or far away.)

_____

_____

_____

_____

Sometimes I live out of performance and fear of disappointing God or people. I often struggle with questions, thoughts, and feelings such as... (Can you recall a time when you felt as though you disappointed someone or even God? Describe it here.)

_____

_____

_____

_____

_____

Now, as I am in the middle of my everyday spiritual routine, here comes a man who seems familiar to me, yet I do not fully recognize Him. He is wearing work clothes, and from the calluses on His hands, He appears to be a man who knows how to work. His presence and face are strong and confident. He is a carpenter. He walks with purpose, knowing what He is doing and where He is going. Now I realize that He is Jesus! As Jesus approaches me, I feel...because...

_____

_____

_____

_____

_____

There is an invitation in His eyes. He is going somewhere and wants me to follow Him. As I get up from my usual spiritual place, I hurry to catch up to Jesus. Jesus never stops moving. I remember that it is the Sabbath, and I must go where He is going to a place of the Rest—a place to connect with Him.

Each step carries me farther away from all that feels usual and safe, and with each step I grow closer to Jesus. I am going to have to trust Him. I have nothing with me—no food or extra clothing. Wherever Jesus is going has to be safe for me. With each step, I feel...because...

All the while, I have been walking behind Jesus, but now just when I get used to seeing the back of His head, Jesus stops and looks back at me over His shoulder. Then He turns fully around and sees me eye-to-eye. As He looks at me eye-to-eye, I feel...because...

Then, with great tenderness and purpose, Jesus asks me, "What are you looking for?—What seems to be missing?" The words touch me deep inside. I don't know quite what to say. It is a simple and obvious question, but leaves me standing flatly on my feet. He didn't ask me for an opinion. He asked me what I was looking for. What have I been looking for...longing for...

As Jesus asks me this question, my heart settles into a simpler and sharper focus. Now as I stand face-to-face with Jesus, all of the many questions that had turned over my heart slip into the background and become one question: "Rabbi, where are we going?" I want to go where He is going. Now His eyes lift up ever so slightly in a smile. There is excitement in His expression, as though He had been waiting for someone to ask just this question, "Where do you live?" With a voice which is settled and confident Jesus says, "Come and see—come and stay with Me for the Rest!" As Jesus invites me, I feel...because...

_____

_____

_____

_____

_____

_____

_____

_____

_____

_____

_____

Now Jesus has set out for His home, and I have joined Him on the journey, talking along the way. I am no longer walking behind Him, but Jesus has slowed His pace so that I am now alongside Him. As the conversation continues, Jesus asks about me—just small talk. I hear Him asking me...I answer Him...

_____

_____

_____

_____

_____

He is interested—He listens! All the while Jesus' steps are certain and deliberate, as if each step was a precious possession—something to be savored. He knows where we are going and leads the way. Along the way I see... (Describe the landscape as you walk along with Jesus. What do you see? This is just a way to make your journey more experiential.)

_____

_____

_____

_____

_____

Now we are getting closer to the place where Jesus lives. We slow down and approach His house. To me Jesus' house looks like... (Describe what you picture in your mind's eye about Jesus' house. There are no right or wrong answers, just what you see.)

_____

_____

_____

_____

_____

_____

_____

As I approach the house where Jesus lives, I feel...because...It makes me want to...

_____

_____

_____

_____

Jesus looks at me and, speaking in a low and compassionate voice, says, "You are going to like this. This is what you have longed for—what you were created for." We take the final steps of the journey to Jesus' home and come to a stop at His door.

Now, standing at the door of the house where He lives, Jesus extends His callused hand, bending down and slightly forward in a gesture of invitation. Looking inside I can see that His home is simple—not pretentious, but warm and inviting. Jesus steps through the door and opens His home to me. There are no waiting servants there—no other people or attendants, just the two of us. It is as if the house is expecting us. As my eyes adjust to the light, I see a few small clay oil lamps providing a gentle, flickering light. In that warm light, a single piece of furniture is revealed, a simple table made from the dark, smooth wood of an olive tree. The table is set with a few round loaves of barley bread and a vessel filled with wine. Now Jesus says, "I made this table with My own hands for just this purpose. Come—Come and Rest with me."

WHAT IS ON YOUR FEET?

Now just inside the door of this one-room dwelling is a small stool also made by Jesus' own hands. As we step inside, Jesus invites me to sit on the stool. We had walked some distance and our feet were covered with the dust of the day. Our feet must be washed. This is usually the task of the lowest servant. But Jesus, the Lamb, wants to wash my feet! As I sit down on the stool I feel...because...

_____

_____

_____

_____

I settle onto the stool and Jesus unties my shoes and puts them aside. Jesus gets up and walks away for a moment but returns with a basin of clean water. Wrapping a towel around His waist, Jesus kneels at my feet and looks up into my eyes to determine whether I am willing to place my feet in the basin. I am reluctant. How could this be proper to allow Jesus to serve me in the most menial way? I should be washing His feet. Then Jesus says, "I did not come to be served, but to serve and give." I cautiously nod my head to Jesus, who looks up at me and begins to pour water on my feet. As the water courses over my feet, I think of the long journey—not just the journey of this day, but of all the previous days of my spiritual journey. As I reflect on my spiritual journey, certain days or events come to mind, such as...

_____

_____

_____

_____

_____

_____

_____

_____

_____

With each application of water, the dust and debris of the journey is being washed away. There have been thoughts that have distracted me along the way—things I worry about. Jesus begins to tell me what He is washing off my feet—the things that worry and take my attention from Him. In truth, anything I worry about is mere dust. These are things I think are important. Jesus is washing these things from my feet...Each worry that Jesus washes off, I release to Him saying... (There may be several concerns that Jesus brings to mind. List each worry that He brings to mind and let Him wash them off your feet.)

"Jesus, I release this dust to You, and I hear You telling me..."

_____

_____

_____

_____

_____

_____

_____

_____

_____

_____

Each issue Jesus has washed away prepares me to be present with Him in this moment. Now that Jesus has washed away the dust of worry and distraction, I hear Him saying to me...

_____

_____

_____

_____

_____

_____

_____

_____

_____

_____

_____

_____

_____

As the dust is removed, I become aware of the immediate moment with my feet in the basin and the hands of Jesus. Jesus takes the towel from around His waist and dries my feet, telling me that as often as I need Him to He will wash my feet. Nothing is as important or valuable as my being present with Him. That is why He invited me into the journey.

WHAT IS IN YOUR HANDS?

Now with my feet dry, I stand up and turn toward the center of the room to see the simple table before me. Jesus walks around to the other side of the table and spreads out His hands in a gesture of invitation for me to join Him. At once I feel excitement and longing, as if there is a place prepared just for me, that without me at the table something would be out of place or missing.

As I focus on the table I feel the heaviness of life that I carried to His table. Jesus begins to look at my hands as if I am carrying something in them. These are the things I thought I had to bring to the table to earn a place there—things and services I have performed instead of coming to that simple table, the realm of rest and connection. Jesus says only a word, "Come!"

As I come, I realize that anything I bring to His table will be a distraction and unnecessary. Jesus begins to tell me what is in my hands—what I have been trying to bring to the table instead of receiving His gift of grace. As He reveals what I have carried, I open my hands and release these burdens to Jesus, saying...

"Jesus, I release _____ into Your hands and come to Your table because You have prepared a place for me there..."

_____

_____

_____

_____

Now that my hands are empty, Jesus takes one of the loaves of bread from the table and speaks a blessing, *"Blessed is the Lord our God King and Creator of all who brought forth this bread from the earth."* Jesus broke off a piece of bread and handed it to me saying, "This is My table and My bread. I have always wanted you at My table. Remember whose table this is and remember Me. Your life, like this bread, is in My hands. *And just as My Father has given Me a Kingdom, I now give you a permanent invitation to eat and drink at My table in My Kingdom."* As Jesus speaks these words, I feel... because...

_____

_____

_____

_____

_____

_____

_____

_____

_____

_____

_____

_____

WHAT IS IN YOUR HEART?

As I settle to my place at the table, I become aware that Jesus and I are sitting at a heart level across from each other. Jesus retrieves a small clay lamp and lights it with the flame of the other lamps already burning. Jesus lifts His face to look at me and begins to speak a blessing over me and the lamp saying, *"Bless this light and the table it rests upon that the whole world would be filled with its light."*

Then Jesus takes a cup of wine in His right hand and blesses it saying, "Let the earth be filled with the glory of Heaven and new life from the fruit of the Vine." Then He breaks off a piece of challah bread and blesses it saying, "This is My body broken and given to bring all men to My table." We eat and drink the bread and wine together. As I take the bread and wine, I feel...because...

_____

_____

_____

_____

As I sit at His table, there is a conversation going on in my heart. I am aware that Jesus sees into my heart and hears that conversation. He knows what drains me and what fulfills me. He knows where I operate in fear or peace. He knows when I feel dragged, pushed, or invited. Because I was created by Him, Jesus knows where my anxious thoughts come from. These are the questions that arise in my heart at the table with Jesus. As the questions arise, Jesus answers them one by one.

My heart asks...

_____

Jesus answers my heart saying...

_____

_____

My heart asks...

_____

Jesus answers my heart saying...

_____

_____

My heart asks...

_____

Jesus answers my heart saying...

_____

_____

My heart asks...

_____

Jesus answers my heart saying...

_____

_____

As I am at the table with Jesus, He says, *"You cannot live by bread alone, but by what I am breathing into your life."* Now I ask Jesus, "Lord, where am I living for mere "bread," serving myself? Where and when do I push back from the table of Your presence? Where do I not trust you to continually breathe Your life into me?" I hear Him saying...

_____

_____

_____

_____

_____

_____

_____

Another and different kind of question comes to my heart. "Lord, what do You like about me? How did You create me differently from everyone else?" I hear Him reply...

_____

_____

_____

_____

_____

_____

_____

_____

_____

_____

_____

_____

_____

_____

_____

_____

WHAT IS IN YOUR EYES?

I am coming to hear Jesus more clearly as I sit at the table. My feet are clean, my hands are empty, and my heart is becoming connected. I am feeling...because...

_____

_____

_____

_____

As I sit across the table from Jesus, I am aware that there is something on the table between us—a large mirror. It is a mirror made of beaten and polished metal which provides a distorted, uneven reflection of me. I want to see Jesus, but the mirror is in the way. I hear Jesus saying, "You do not see yourself or Me clearly. I want us to see each other face-to-face. Now that you've come to the table, you look at this mirror and become a slave to it all over again. I want to see your face."

Jesus takes the mirror and faces it toward me so that I can see how uneven and inaccurate its reflection really is. In the mirror I focus on myself and compare myself.

As poor as that reflection is, I often look at my reflection and compare myself with other people. I cannot see them accurately either as the mirror is always there in the way. When I look into the mirror, I also see my past sins and mistakes—where I've lived away from the table on my own. The most painful things I look at in the mirror are past wounds and hurts—where I've been betrayed or abandoned.

As Jesus shows me the deception of the mirror, it is obvious that He wants to heal the lies and wounds from the past that keep me from seeing Him. Now I look into the mirror and ask Jesus, "Lord, where and how do I compare myself to other people?" Jesus responds by bringing this to my heart... (There may be several things Jesus brings to mind. List them all.)

_____

_____

_____

_____

_____

_____

_____

_____

_____

_____

_____

_____

Looking sad, Jesus begins to show me sins and mistakes from the past when I lived away from His table. I had already asked and received forgiveness and cleansing for these sins, but have not yet released them to Him. They are still between my face and His. Each time I grow closer to Him, they come back to the mirror and I see them instead of Jesus. These are the sins that keep me living in the mirror rather than at His table face-to-face...

There is more healing now for me as Jesus reminds me of wounds from the past that are not yet healed and the lies and distortions that came with them. Jesus now takes the mirror in His hands. With each wound and hurt, I realize that Jesus holds the mirror and that the hurts and the ones who hurt me are in His hands. I forgive each one Jesus shows me in the mirror. With each healing, Jesus reminds me that there is a place for me at His table so that I am safe to forgive. These are the wounds Jesus shows me...

_____

_____

_____

_____

_____

Now Jesus puts the mirror aside and says, "You are mine. I love you. I am your peace and rest. You are My beloved, and I am pleased with who you are and who you are becoming. Be present here with Me. Here is how I see you..."

_____

_____

_____

_____

_____

With the mirror off the table and His words freshly breathed into me, my face begins to reflect His light as He sits opposite me at the table. I will never live in shame again. I am being changed and transformed to look like Jesus. He is making me His reflection.

As I have received His truth I feel...because...

_____

_____

_____

_____

What is in your life? Though we have come to the table with Christ and experienced the rich feast of His grace, there are influences in our lives that want to draw us back into the world. The Lord has made it possible for us to live in a place of Rest, carrying all the table represents with us.

BEING HIS FRAGRANCE

Now I sit at Jesus' table with clean feet, empty hands, and a focused and healed heart. I lay down in a place Jesus prepared just for me and sleep. As I sleep, His love and truth soak into and surround me. When I wake up, this time of the Rest is coming to an end. Jesus says, "I want to give you peace that you can live with all the time. You can live from your place at My table." With that, Jesus produces a small box as plain and simple as the house and His table. It has several small holes on the top. Jesus smiles and shakes this little box and smells it, breathing deeply, then hands it to me. The box is filled with fragrant spices like cinnamon and cloves. It is the fragrance of the Rest.[1]

Jesus said, "This will remind you of the Rest you have in Me. Breathe it in—remember Me—remember that you live now from My table. When you encounter the dust of your daily life, remember this fragrance of Rest. When you pick up something into your hand and are tempted to try to impress Me to earn your place at My table, remember this fragrance of Rest. When you sit at My table and feel weary or afraid, remember this fragrance of Rest. And because you still live in this world with people who don't know Me or don't know they have a place at My table, you will be hurt sometimes. Become My fragrance of Rest, even to those who hurt you. Love them—forgive them—release them."

With that, Jesus shares a little more bread and wine and says, "This is for the journey. As you take it into your body, remember your place at My table and the Rest, and I will be with you always and everywhere. I am what you have been looking for—this is where I live—Come."

ENDNOTE

1. This is the havdalah part of the Sabbath tradition when the family sits at the table and passes around a small box that is filled with fragrant spices. In this way those at the table will carry the fragrance of Rest with them to remind them and sustain them until the next Sabbath.

MINISTRY INFORMATION

The mission of Grace and Truth Fellowship, Inc., is to transform local churches into healing centers. Serving as president of this ministry, Thom Gardner is available as a speaker/teacher for seminars, conferences, or other extended meetings. Grace and Truth Fellowship, Inc., also offers the Healing the Wounded Heart Training Seminar to equip the local church to bring healing to wounded hearts. The purpose of the seminar is to help participants find personal freedom through confrontation of their own past wounds, and then equip them to bring healing to others.

Healing the Wounded Heart Training Seminar is a three-day seminar that covers the material in this book and offers instruction and practice in the facilitation of this approach to healing wounded hearts. Our goal is to multiply, rather than monopolize, this approach to the ministry of inner healing.

If you are interested in attending a Healing the Wounded Heart Training Seminar, contact Grace and Truth Fellowship, Inc., at 717-263-6869, or see our Web site at www.graceandtruthfellowship.com.

ALSO BY THOM GARDNER

Turned Toward Mercy